Burmese phrasebook
3rd edition – October 2001
First published – April 1988

Published by
Lonely Planet Publications Pty Ltd, ABN 36 005 607 983
90 Maribyrnong St, Footscray, Victoria 3011, Australia

Lonely Planet Offices
Australia Locked Bag 1, Footscray, Victoria 3011
USA 150 Linden St, Oakland CA 94607
UK 10a Spring Place, London NW5 3BH
France 1 rue du Dahomey, 75011 Paris

Cover illustration
Ferry, Irrawaddy by Julian Chapple

ISBN 1 74059 048 1

text © Lonely Planet Publications Pty Ltd 2001
cover illustration © Lonely Planet Publications Pty Ltd 2001

Printed by Colorcraft Ltd, Hong Kong

This Edition

This edition was updated and expanded by Vicky Bowman. Vicky studied Burmese at the School of Oriental and African Studies in London and lived in Myanmar for three years from 1990 to 1993. In her spare time, she translates modern Burmese writing.

Thanks to Aung Maw Zin, Moe Moe Hnin and Anna Allott for assisting in checking proofs.

Thanks also to David Bradley, who, with Vicky Bowman and San San Hnin Tun, updated and expanded the previous Burmese phrasebook, from which this edition developed.

From the Publisher

This book is the product of a small but diligent team: Sally Steward oversaw the project early on; Ingrid Seebus got the ball rolling; and Peter D'Onghia stepped in to take control of the Grammar and Pronunciation chapters and to look over the preliminary layout. Karina Coates supervised the entire project and played a vital role in the late stages of production; Emma Koch lent her technical expertise; Sophie Putman busied herself editing and proofing; Chris Waddington solved many a script problem, enabling the whole book to go ahead; Yukiyoshi Kamimura created the impressive illustrations, as well as perfecting the layout, which Fabrice Rocher cheerfully checked; Julian Chapple supplied the inspired cover design; and Natasha Velleley took responsibility for the map.

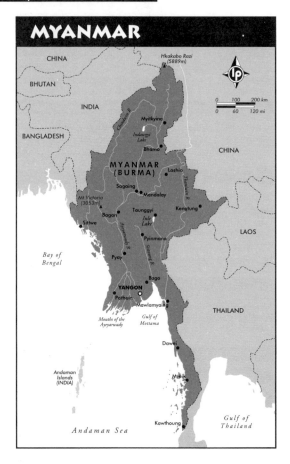

MYANMAR

CHINA

BHUTAN

Hkakabo Razi
(5889m)

INDIA

BANGLADESH

Chindwin R.

Myitkyina

Indawgyi
Lake

Bhamo

CHINA

MYANMAR
(BURMA)

Lashio

Salween R.

Sagaing

Mandalay

Kengtung

Mt Victoria
(3053m)

Taunggyi

Bagan

Inle
Lake

LAOS

Ayeyarwady R.

Sittwe

Pyinmana

Bay of
Bengal

Pyay

Sittang R.

Bago

YANGON

Pathein

Mawlamyaing

Mouth of the
Ayeyarwady

Gulf of
Mottama

THAILAND

Dawei

Andaman
Islands
(INDIA)

Myeik

Andaman Sea

Kawthoung

Gulf of
Thailand

0   100   200 km
0   60   120 mi

INTRODUCTION

Burmese is in the Tibeto-Burman language family, as are most of the languages of Myanmar (Burma) and many in neighbouring China, India, Thailand and Nepal. As the national language, it has over 40 million speakers, more than 30 million of whom use it as their first language. This means that Burmese has more speakers than any other Tibeto-Burman language, including Tibetan.

After Tibetan, Burmese was one of the earliest Tibeto-Burman languages to develop a writing system. The earliest surviving inscription, known as the Rajakumar after the person who had it prepared, is at the Myazedi in Bagan (Pagan). It dates from 1112 AD and is in four languages: Pali, Mon, Pyu and Burmese.

Burmese has some minor dialect differences; the standard dialect is that of Mandalay and Yangon, which is spoken throughout the central area of Myanmar, and taught in schools everywhere. Rakhine (Arakanese) in the west and Tavoyan in the south are slightly different, while Intha (spoken by the people of Inle Lake), Yaw, Danu and Taungyo are more divergent. There are many other languages spoken in Myanmar, some of them in the same language family and others quite unrelated. Nevertheless, Burmese is spoken by nearly everyone in the country; and widespread literacy has been achieved through schools and adult literacy programmes.

Like many other languages, Burmese has two varieties: one is used in writing and associated formal activities; the other is used in speaking and other informal situations. The main differences are in vocabulary, especially the most frequent words and particles; for example 'this' is **di** in spoken Burmese, but **i** in the written language. Everything in this phrasebook is the informal spoken variety, which is appropriate for all situations a traveller is likely to encounter.

MYANMAR OR BURMA?

Since 1989, the government has preferred the literary form Myanmar to refer to the country, its language and its people as a whole. (The former English name 'Burma' is derived from the spoken form.) The English name for many other places and groups was also changed in 1989. In this phrasebook, we use Burmese to refer to the people and the language (as it is more commonly referred to outside the country) and Myanmar to refer to the country. For place names, the current name is given first, with the former name in brackets; for example, the capital, Yangon (Rangoon); the western state of Rakhine (Arakan); and so on.

THE LANGUAGE

There are 33 consonants in the writing system, and there are traditionally held to be 12 vowel sounds. As in other languages spoken in the region, there are various combinations of consonants; and the vowel sound of each syllable is written by adding one or more symbols above, below, before, or after the consonant that it follows. Additional markings are used to represent the tones. Given the written form, it is almost always possible to know how to pronounce a word, but because of changes in pronunciation over the centuries the reverse is not true.

The spelling used here is the revised spelling introduced in 1980, as formulated by the Myanmar (Burma) Language Commission. The best available bilingual dictionary is their Myanmar-English Dictionary published in 1993. Various English-Burmese dictionaries are available, none of them very effective. The Students' English-English/Myanmar Dictionary from SAM Translation Services, also published in 1993, is fairly comprehensive but targeted at Burmese speakers learning English. None of these is convenient to carry around, but the available pocket dictionaries like the Thalun have many gaps. Also, note that nearly all of these dictionaries focus primarily or exclusively on written language. If you are serious about learning Burmese, you may want to get one of the better monolingual dictionaries, such as the one-volume 1991 or five-volume 1980 dictionaries of the Myanmar Language Commission.

Many Burmese nouns are borrowed from English, though the meaning and sound may be somewhat different. If you are totally stumped, you can try the English noun in the middle of a Burmese sentence and this may sometimes work. There are also some loan words from Hindi. Although much of the more formal vocabulary comes from Pali, the language of Theravada Buddhism, it is pronounced in a Burmese way, and so sounds different from Thai, Sri Lankan or other Pali pronunciation.

Apart from the spoken/written difference, Burmese is not a difficult language. The three tones are less difficult to keep apart than the five tones of Thai or the six tones of Vietnamese, and some effort to produce them will be rewarded by the delight of Burmese people. Other aspects of pronunciation can best be learned by listening and imitation. Enjoy your time in Myanmar, and good luck in speaking the language!

INTRODUCTION

ABBREVIATIONS USED IN THIS BOOK

adj	adjective	n	noun
adv	adverb	pl	plural
f	feminine	sg	singular
lit	literally	v	verb
m	masculine		

HOW TO USE THIS PHRASEBOOK
You *Can* Speak Another Language

It's true – anyone can speak another language. Don't worry if you haven't studied languages before, or that you studied a language at school for years and can't remember any of it. It doesn't even matter if you failed English grammar. After all, that's never affected your ability to speak English! And this is the key to picking up a language in another country. You don't need to sit down and memorise endless grammatical details and you don't need to memorise long lists of vocabulary. You just need to start speaking. Once you start you'll be amazed how many prompts you'll get to help you build on those first words. You'll hear people speaking, pick up sounds from TV, catch a word or two that you think you know from the local radio, see something on a billboard - all these things help to build your understanding.

Plunge In

There's just one thing you need to start speaking another language – courage. Your biggest hurdle is overcoming the fear of saying aloud what may seem to you to be just a bunch of sounds.

The best way to start overcoming your fear is to memorise a few key words and phrases that you know you'll be saying again and again. A standard greeting is one of the most useful: min-gǎla-ba, literally 'It's a blessing', is good for any formal situation and in cities; while 'Are you well?', ne-kaùn-yéh-là, is fine for any informal encounter. You can reply ne-kaùn-ba-deh, 'I am well'. Here's an important hint though – right from the beginning, learn at least one phrase that will be useful but not essential. Try 'Pleased to meet you', **twé-yá-da wùn-tha-ba-deh**, or 'I like it here', **di-hma ăyàn-pyaw-ne-deh**, or even a conversational piece like 'It's very hot today', **di-né theiq pu-deh** (people everywhere love to talk about the weather). Having this extra phrase will enable you to move away from the basics and, when you get a reply and a smile, it'll also boost your confidence. You'll find that people you speak to will like it too, as they'll understand that at least you've tried to learn more of the language than just the usual essential words.

Ways to Remember
There are several ways to learn a language. Most people find they learn from a variety of these, although people usually have a preferred way to remember. Some like to see the written word and remember the sound from what they see. Some like to just hear it spoken in context (if this is you, try talking to yourself in Burmese, but do it in the car or somewhere private, to give yourself confidence, and so others don't wonder about your sanity!).

Others, especially the more mathematically inclined, like to analyse the grammar of a language, and piece together words according to the rules of grammar. The very visually inclined like to associate the written word and even sounds with some visual stimulus, such as from illustrations, TV and general things they see in the street. As you learn, you'll discover what works best for you – be aware of what made you really remember a particular word, and if it sticks in your mind, keep using that method.

Kicking Off
Chances are you'll want to learn some of the language before you go. The first thing to do is to memorise those essential phrases and words. Check out the basics (page 41) ... and don't forget your extra phrase. Try the sections on making conversation (page 54) or greeting people (page 42) for a phrase you'd like to use. Write some of these words down on a separate piece of paper

and stick them up around the place. On the fridge, by the bed, on your computer, as a bookmark – somewhere where you'll see them often. Try putting some words in context – the 'How much is it?', **beh-lauq-lèh?**, note, for instance, could go in your wallet.

If you have time, other useful words to memorise are the numbers (page 153) and some key verbs (page 30). At this stage, don't worry about your pronunciation or getting the grammar right – just take the plunge and start speaking.

I Have a Flat Tyre

Doesn't seem like the phrase you're going to need? Well in fact, it could be very useful. As are all the phrases in this book, provided you have the courage to mix and match them. We have given specific examples within each section. But the key words remain the same even when the situation changes. While you may not be planning on any cycling during your trip, the first part of the phrase 'I have a …' could refer to anything else, and there are words in the dictionary that, we hope, will fit your needs. So whether it's a 'ticket', 'visa' or 'headache', you'll be able to put the words together to convey your meaning.

Finally

Don't be concerned if you feel you can't memorise words. On the inside front and back covers are the most essential words and phrases you'll need. You could also try tagging a few pages for other key phrases.

PRONUNCIATION

Burmese is not a difficult language to pronounce, although the tones and some of the consonants may seem difficult at first. The best way to overcome this is to listen to the way native speakers differentiate between the tones.

The Burmese pronunciation used here is the same as that used in the textbooks by Okell, the most up-to-date Burmese course available.

VOWELS

Burmese vowel sounds should be easy for speakers of English and other European languages. They occur in open, nasalised and stopped forms. Tones also affect the way vowels are constructed (see page 21).

open	pronunciation
i	as the 'i' in 'marine'
e	as the 'e' in 'hey'
eh	as the 'e' in 'bet'
a	as the 'a' in 'father'
aw	as the 'aw' in British 'law'
o	as the 'o' in 'go'
u	as the 'oo' in 'zoo'

PRONUNCIATION

Nasalisation of vowels is like that found in French. Speakers of English or other languages can approximate this by putting a weak 'n' at the end of such a syllable. This nasalisation is indicated by n after the vowel, as in ein, 'house'.

nasalised	pronunciation
in	as the 'in' in 'sin'
ein	as the 'ain' in 'pain'
an	as the 'an' in 'man'
oun	as the 'oan' in 'moan'
un	as the 'un' in 'junta'
ain	as the 'ine' in 'line'
aun	as the 'own' in 'brown'

The stopped vowels are pronounced as short syllables, cut off at the end by a sharp catch in the voice (a glottal stop). See opposite for more information about stopped syllables.

stopped	pronunciation
iq	as the 'it' in 'sit'
eiq	as the 'ate' in 'late'
eq	as the 'et' in 'bet'
aq	as the 'at' in 'mat'
ouq	as the 'oat' in 'boat'
uq	as the 'oot' in 'foot'
aiq	as the 'ight' in 'might'
auq	as the 'out' in 'stout'

TONES

Burmese tones are largely a matter of relative stress between adjoining syllables. They exist in English too: think about the different stresses, and hence meaning, between 'He's thought less' and 'He's thoughtless'.

Every syllable has one of five alternatives: creaky high tone; plain high tone; low tone; stopped syllable; or reduced (weak) syllable. In Burmese, the tone of a word can change its meaning (see the following examples). However, note that the tone of a word may change depending on the surrounding words.

PRONUNCIATION

Creaky High Tone

This is made with the voice tense, producing a high-pitched and relatively short creaky sound, such as occurs with the English words 'heart' and 'squeak'. It is indicated by an acute accent over the vowel, for example ká, 'dance'.

Plain High Tone

The pitch of the voice starts quite high, then falls for a fairly long time, similar to the pronunciation of words like 'squeal', 'car' and 'way'. It is indicated by a grave accent over the vowel, for example kà which, conveniently, is the Burmese word for 'car'.

Low Tone

The voice is relaxed, stays at a low pitch for a fairly long time, and does not rise or fall in pitch. It is indicated by no accent over the vowel, for example ka, 'shield'.

Stopped Syllable

This is a very short syllable, on a high pitch, cut off at the end by a sharp catch in the voice (a glottal stop). This is like the sound, 'uh-oh', or the Cockney pronunciation of 't' in a word like 'bottle'. If you have trouble with this sound, try replacing it with a 't', but keep the syllable short. It is indicated in this book by a q after the vowel, for example kaq, 'join'. However, the q is not pronounced.

PRONUNCIATION

Reduced (Weak) Syllable

This is a shortened syllable, usually the first syllable of a two-syllable word, which is said without stress, like the first syllable of 'again' in English. Only the vowel 'a', sometimes preceded by a consonant, occurs in a reduced syllable – this is indicated by a ˘ above the vowel, eg, ălouq, 'work'. Any syllable but the last in a word can be reduced.

CONSONANTS

Consonants only occur at the beginning of a syllable – there are no consonants that occur after the vowel. The consonants b, d, j, g, m, n, ng, sh, h, z, w, l, y are pronounced as in English. Note that the w sound can occur on its own, or in combinations with other consonants, and that the g is hard, as the 'g' in 'gate'. The following consonants may cause confusion:

th	as the 'th' in 'thin'
dh	as the 'th' in 'the' or 'their'
ny	as the 'ny' in 'canyon'
hm, hn, hny, hng, hl	made with a puff of air just before the 'm', 'n' or 'l'
p', t', s', c', k'	aspirated (see below)
p, t, s, c, k	unaspirated (see below)

Aspirated Consonants

The aspirated sounds p', t', s', c', k' are made with a puff of air after the sound; this is the way the letters 'p', 't', 'k' are pronounced in English at the beginning of a word. The unaspirated sounds p, t, s, c, k are without this puff of air, as the letters 'p', 't', 'k' sound in English after an 's' as in 'spin', 'stir' and 'skin'.

The unaspirated c and aspirated c' are similar to English 'ch' as in 'church'. Remember that sh as in 'ship', s as in 'sip', and the aspirated s'are three different sounds. Another difficulty is in saying the ng at the beginning of a syllable – try saying 'hang on', then leave off the 'ha' to get an idea of the sound.

Like most languages, Burmese sounds different when spoken rapidly. One change which happens even in slow speech is that the aspirated and unaspirated sounds p', p; t', t; s', s; c', c and k', k within a word change into the voiced sounds b, d, z, j and g, and the th sound changes into the voiced sound dh. This happens automatically to the consonant when it appears at the beginning of the second, third or later syllable in a word, unless the syllable before it is a stopped syllable. For example:

yauq-cà	'man'	the c does not become j because of the stopped syllable
yì-zà	'girlfriend'	the original s becomes z

To distinguish between voiced and unvoiced sounds, first distinguish between 's' (as in 'bus' or 'sip') and 'z' (as in 'buzz' or 'zip'). Place two fingers on your throat as you pronounce these words and you'll feel a vibration with the 'z' but not with the 's'. The position of your tongue and lips remain the same for both the 'z' sound and the 's' sound, but the vibration distinguishes the two. This vibration is known as 'voicing'.

TRANSLITERATION

As noted earlier, the Burmese pronunciation used here is the same as that used in the textbooks by Okell, the most up-to-date Burmese course available. Transliterated syllables (with the exception of the reduced syllable ă) have been separated by hyphens and breaks between words, or groups of words, by spaces. This is intended to make it easier for the learner. However, native speakers often do not speak with a clear division between words or syllables.

Note that other transliteration systems use different letters to represent the sounds. Aspirated consonants, represented here by k', s', t' and p', may instead be spelled with an 'h' before or after the consonant. A creaky tone may be indicated by a final 't', eg, Hpakant (in Kachin State).

Various combinations of letters may be used to represent the same vowel sound: **e** and **eh** are both often transliterated as 'ay'; **ain** may be represented as 'aing', **auq** as 'auk', and so on. For these reasons and because the official English forms of many placenames changed in 1989, the Burmese versions of common placenames and tourist sites are given on pages 131-132.

Although there is traditionally no 'r' in Burmese, it appears in some loan words, such as **re-di-yo** 'radio' or **da-reiq-s'an** 'animal' (Pali). Sometimes it is replaced with a **y**. Similarly there is no 'f' or 'v' in Burmese; loan words containing these consonants often use **p'** and **b** respectively.

In Burmese script, the sounds **c**, **c'**, **j** are written using the Burmese letters for **k**, **k'**, **g** plus **y** or **r**, so romanised forms of Burmese often represent them as **ky**, **gy** and so on. One example is the unit of currency, **caq**, which is usually written 'kyat' in the Roman alphabet, although pronounced like 'chat' (see page 92).

However, if you pronounce things the way they are written in this phrasebook, you should be understood. If this doesn't work, try showing the written version of what you want, and people will say it for you.

BURMESE SCRIPT
Vowels
Each vowel is written using a symbol or combination of symbols above, below, before or after the consonant that it follows. Tones also affect the way vowels are constructed. The box opposite shows the symbols used in each case, with the hyphen representing the bearer consonant.

To prevent confusion with other consonants, there is some-times more than one way of writing the same vowel. For example, if you added ာ (a) to ပ (p), it would become ပာ, which is the same symbol as for h, so instead it is written as ပါ.

Creaky High		Low		Plain High	
ー	á	‐ာː ‐ါː	à	‐ာ ‐ါ	a
◌ိ	í	◌ီː	ì	◌ီ	i
‐ု	ú	‐ူː	ù	‐ူ	u
ေ‐	é	ေ‐ː	è	ေ‐	e
‐ဲ	éh	‐ဲ	èh	‐ဲ	eh
‐ို	ó	‐ိုː	ò	‐ို	o
ေ‐ာ်	áw	ေ‐ာ ေ‐ါ	àw	ေ‐ာ် ေ‐ါ်	aw

PRONUNCIATION

The box below shows the vowels in their nasalised and stopped forms. The different forms here indicate whether the nasalised/stopped vowel is based on n (န), m (မ), p (ပ) or t (တ).

Nasalised		Stopped	
‐ဉ် ‐င်	in	‐စ်	iq
◌ိဉ် ◌ိင်	ein	◌ိစ် ◌ိဉ်	eiq
		‐က်	eq
‐န် ‐မ် ◌ဲ	an	‐တ် ‐ပ်	aq
‐ုန် ‐ုမ် ◌ု	oun	‐ုတ် ‐ုပ်	ouq
◌ုန် ◌ုမ် ◌ု	un	◌ုတ် ◌ုပ်	uq
◌ိုဉ် ◌ိုင်	ain	◌ိုဉ်	aiq
ေ‐ာင်	aun	ေ‐ာက်	auq

Consonants

The box below lists the 33 Burmese consonants.

Character	Pronunciation	Character	Pronunciation
က	ká	ဒ	dá
ခ	k'a	ဓ	dá
ဂ	gá	န	ná
ဃ	gá	ပ	pá
င	ngá	ဖ	p'á
စ	sá	ဗ	bá
ဆ	s'á	ဘ	bá
ဇ	zá	မ	má
ဈ	zá	ယ	yá
ဉ	nyá	ရ	yá
ဋ	tá	လ	lá
ဌ	t'á	ဝ	wá
ဍ	dá	သ	thá
ဎ	dá	ဟ	há
ဏ	ná	ဠ	lá
တ	tá	အ	á
ထ	t'á		

GRAMMAR

The following outline of Burmese grammar is not a complete description, but it gives the basics and shows you how to put together your own phrases and sentences. Once you become familiar with the grammar here, you'll find it easy to learn sentence patterns for specific situations, allowing you to plug in new vocabulary as the need arises.

WORD ORDER
The word order in Burmese is generally subject-object-verb, but may also be object-subject-verb.

I will give you a book.   cǎnaw sa-ouq tǎouq pè-meh (m)
                              (lit: I book one-book give-meh)
I will give you this book.   di sa-ouq cǎnaw pè-meh (m)
                              (lit: this book I give-meh)

Unlike English, which has prepositions and modal verbs such as 'will' before the verb, particles in Burmese are placed after the word that they belong with.

He will be able to go   thu yan-goun-go thwà-nain-meh
    to Yangon (Rangoon).   (lit: he Yangon-to go-can-meh)

GRAMMATICAL TERMS

A number of basic grammatical terms are used in this chapter:

adjective	adds information about a noun *red* wine
adverb	adds information about a verb or adjective He runs *quickly*. *very* big
conjunction	joins together sentences or parts of a sentence Wash the car *and* walk the dog.
noun	a person (*John*), thing (*book*), place (*beach*) or idea (*happiness*)
object	refers to the noun or pronoun that is affected by the verb Paul washes *the dog*.
preposition	introduces information about location, place or direction *at* the market
pronoun	usually takes the place of a noun *he* sings instead of Paul sings
subject	refers to the noun or pronoun that is performing an action *The man* washes the dog.
verb	an action or doing word He *runs* fast.

GRAMMAR

ARTICLES

There is no article corresponding to 'the' or 'a/an'.

NOUNS

Each noun has only one form. You can show that something is plural by adding t(w)e/d(w)e (the w can be omitted) after the noun. However, it isn't always necessary to add t(w)e/d(w)e – it just makes it clearer.

with the children	k'ălè-dwe-néh *or* k'ălè-de-néh
	(lit: child-plural-with)

One of the main differences between Burmese and English grammar is that, providing it is clear what is being said, a noun may simply be left out without having to be replaced by a pronoun. However, it is probably easier – and less likely to lead to misunderstanding – to leave the nouns and pronouns in.

The main noun particles, which come after the noun they relate to, are as follows:

to	ko/go
from (places)	ká/gá
from (people)	s'i-gá
with	néh
at/in/on	hma

If you want to distinguish between the subject and object of the sentence, add ká/gá to the end of the subject and ko/go to the end of the object.

Father gives a book to	ăp'e-gá thămì-go ein-hma
his daughter at home.	sa-ouq pè-deh
	(lit: father-gá daughter-go
	home-at book gives)

Where noun particles have two forms (eg, twe/dwe and ko/go), it is the preceding syllable that determines which form (voiced or non-voiced) to use. Unless the preceding syllable is stopped (eg, taq), the following syllable is 'voiced' and begins with 'g', 'd', 'b' etc. Voicing happens naturally: for example, it is easier to say kà-go than kà-ko. For more information about voicing, see Pronunciation, page 19.

PRONOUNS

There are many different pronouns in Burmese, but you can get by with just a few. Listed below are the polite forms for use with people you don't know very well. One unusual feature is that the sex of the speaker determines which pronoun is used for 'I', 'we', 'you' (sg) and 'you' (pl).

	male speaker		female speaker	
I	cănaw	ကျွန်တော်	cămá	ကျွန်မ
you (sg)	k'ămyà	ခင်ဗျား	shin	ရှင်
he/she/it	thu	သူ	thu	သူ
we	cănaw-dó	ကျွန်တော်တို့	cămá-dó	ကျွန်မတို့
you (pl)	k'ămyà-dó	ခင်ဗျားတို့	shin-dó	ရှင်တို့
they	thu-dó	သူတို့	thu-dó	သူတို့

A man uses cănaw for himself and k'ămyà for 'you', but a woman uses cămá for herself and shin for 'you'.

If you want to make a pronoun into a plural, attach dó to it, eg, cămá-dó, 'we'. However, often speakers will use just thu rather than thu-dó to mean 'they'.

Very often a person's title, occupation or kinship can be used to signify 'you' or 'I', for example:

older man	ù-lè (lit: uncle)	ဦးလေး
older woman	daw-daw (lit: auntie)	ဒေါ်ဒေါ်
man (same age)	ko-ko (lit: big brother)	ကိုကို
woman (same age)	má-má (lit: big sister)	မမ
professional person (m)	s'ăya (lit: teacher)	ဆရာ
professional person (f)	s'ăya-má (lit: teacher)	ဆရာမ

Although the term s'ăya/s'ăya-má literally means 'teacher', it is also used as a term of respect. Visitors of all occupations may find that this is the way they are addressed.

GRAMMAR

As noted earlier, pronouns can be left out altogether if the meaning is clear.

(I) want to go   thwà-jin-deh
                               (lit: go-want-deh)

As with nouns (see page 25), various particles can be added to pronouns.

with you (female speaking)	shin-néh
	(lit: you-with)
from him/her	thú-s'i-gá
	(lit: him/her-from)

POSSESSIVES

The possessor precedes the thing that's possessed in Burmese. To indicate possession, either add yéh to the end of the possessor or a creaky high tone on the last syllable of the possessor.

my house	cămá-yéh ein (f)
	(lit: I-yéh house)
daughter's car	thămí kà
	(lit: daughter-creaky-high-tone car)

VERBS

As with nouns and pronouns, particles and other grammatical markers are added to verbs; these particles show things such as tense. In fact, all verbs except for commands have at least one particle attached.

Tense

A particle indicating the tense of the verb occurs in almost every sentence. There are three main tense particles: teh/deh indicates the present and past tense (the context will clarify which); meh indicates the future tense; and pi/bi indicates a completed action. Again, which form to use depends on the preceding syllable (see page 26).

I go./I went.	thwà-deh
	(lit: go-deh)
I have gone.	thwà-bi
	(lit: go-bi)
I will go.	thwà-meh
	(lit: go-meh)
I eat./I ate.	sà-deh
	(lit: eat-deh)
I have eaten.	sà-bi
	(lit: eat-bi)
I will eat.	sà-meh
	(lit: eat-meh)

TO BE

There are several equivalents for the English verb 'to be'.

With adjectives, there is no word for 'to be' (see page 33). It is also quite possible to have no word for 'to be' when two nouns are together, for example:

He/She is a teacher.	**thu s'ăya**
	(lit: he/she teacher)
They are at school.	**thu-dó caùn-hma**
	(lit: they school-at)

However, such a sentence is commonly finished off with the 'politeness' particle, **pa/ba** (see page 39):

He/She is a teacher.	**thu s'ăya-ba**
	(lit: he/she teacher-ba)

Sometimes this kind of sentence uses the verb **p'yiq**, 'to become', but this suggests that something has changed.

He/She is (now) a teacher.	**thu s'ăya p'yiq-teh**
	(lit: he/she teacher become-teh)

Another related verb is **shí** 'to have' or 'to exist', often meaning 'there is/are'.

There is a monastery here.	**di-hma caùn shí-deh**
	(lit: here monastery exists-deh)
I have a car.	**cănaw/cămá kà shí-deh (m/f)**
	(lit: I car have-deh)

A further possibility is ne, 'to be at', 'to live' or 'to stay'. As with p'yiq, the addition of ne suggests a different meaning: they live there, or stay there for some time, rather than just happening to be there now.

They are at school.   thu-dó caùn-hma ne-deh
                             (lit: they school-at are)

Useful Verbs

There are no true infinitives in Burmese, so the verbs listed below are given in the present/past tense.

agree	thăbàw tu-deh
bring	yu-deh
come	la-deh
cost	cá-deh/koun cá-deh
depart (leave)	t'weq-teh
do	louq-teh
eat	t'ămin sà-deh
go	thwà-deh
have	shí-deh
help	ku-nyi-deh
know (someone/something)	thí-deh
know (how to)	taq-teh
like	caiq-teh
make	louq-teh
meet	twé-deh
need	lo-aq-deh
prefer	po caiq-teh
return	pyan-deh
say	pyàw-deh/s'o-deh
see	myin-deh
stay	ne-deh
take	yu-deh
understand	nà-leh-deh
want	lo-jin-deh

MODAL VERBS

There are a number of modal verbs in Burmese – the following
is a list of the most useful ones. Modal verbs generally come after
the verb and before the tense particle.

• **must, have to**	yá
I go.	thwà-deh
	(lit: go-deh)
I had to go.	thwà-yá-deh
	(lit: go-must-deh)
I must go to	cănaw/cămá yan-goun-go
Yangon (Rangoon).	thwà-yá-meh (m/f)
	(lit: I Yangon-to go-must-meh)
• **can (be skilled at)**	taq/daq
The teacher can speak	s'aya băma-zăgà
Burmese.	pyàw-daq-teh
	(lit: teacher burmese-language
	speak-can-teh)
I can speak Burmese.	cănaw/cămá băma-lo
	pyàw-daq-teh (m/f)
	(lit: I burmese-style
	speak-can-teh)
• **can (be physically able)**	nain
I can see the house.	cănaw ein-ko
	myin-nain-deh (m)
	(lit: I house-to see-can-deh)

- **want to**   c'in/jin
  I leave.   t'weq-deh
                                       (lit: leave-deh)

  I want to leave.   t'weq-c'in-deh
                                       (lit: leave-want-deh)

  I eat.   sà-deh
                                       (lit: eat-deh)

  I want to eat.   sà-jin-deh
                                       (lit: eat-want-deh)

  Mother wants to go   ăme yan-goun-go
    to Yangon (Rangoon).   thwà-jin-deh
                                       (lit: mother Yangon-to
                                         go-want-deh)

- **continue** (equivalent to '-ing') ne
  The soldier is riding   siq-thà mì-yăt'à
    on the train.   sì-ne-deh
                                       (lit: soldier train ride-ing-deh)

- **try to**   cí/jí
  Please try to eat some   myăma t'ămìn-hìn
    Burmese food.   sà-jí-ba
                                       (lit: Myanmar rice-curry
                                         eat-try-ba)

- **have ever**   p'ù/bù
  I have never been   băgan mă-yauq-p'ù-bù
    to Bagan (Pagan).   (lit: Bagan mă-arrive-ever-bù)

Note that the modal p'ù/bù, 'have ever', and the second part of the negation, p'ù/bù, are the same (see page 38). However, they can be together in one sentence, as above, creating the negative sense 'have never'.

ADJECTIVES

In Burmese, adjectives work exactly like verbs – they come after the noun, and are followed by various particles. In a sentence where there is an adjective, there is no equivalent of the verb 'to be'; the adjective *is* the verb. The adjective and the tense particle are together referred to as the 'adjective-verb'.

This person is big.	di lu cì-deh
	(lit: this person big-deh)
This car is blue.	di kà pya-deh
	(lit: this car blue-deh)

To put an adjective-verb with a noun in Burmese there are two possibilities: certain colour and size adjectives can be attached to the end of the noun; and any adjective can be put in a relative clause before the noun, the clause being marked by téh/déh between the verb and the following noun.

house	ein
a big house	ein-jì
	(lit: house-big)
a house that is big	cì-déh ein
	(lit: big-déh house)

Comparisons

Comparisons are made by adding po, 'more', to the beginning of the adjective-verb. The word equivalent to 'than' is t'eq and it is placed after the relevant noun.

This room is better than that room.
di ăk'àn ho ăk'àn-t'eq po-kaùn-deh
(lit: this room that room-t'eq more-good-deh)

My car is faster than his/her car
cănaw/cămá-yéh kà thú-kà-t'eq po-myan-deh
(lit: my car his-car-t'eq more-fast-deh)

GRAMMAR

Equivalence, expressed in English by 'the same as', is expressed in Burmese by putting the noun(s), linked by néh (meaning 'and/ with') before ătu-du, or, more emphatically, ătu-du-ba-bèh, 'the very same', for example:

This car is the same as that car.	di kà-néh ho kà-néh ătu-du-ba-bèh (lit: this car-néh that car-néh the-very-same)
It is the same as this one.	di-ha-néh ătu-du-ba-bèh (lit: this-thing-néh the-very-same)

COUNTERS

In Burmese, the number always follows the noun, and is followed by a counter (also known as a classifier), one of a small set of words used in counting. More details on counters are given in the Numbers & Amounts chapter, page 154.

QUESTIONS

There are two types of questions in Burmese: those requiring a 'yes'/'no' answer, and those asking for specific information.

'Yes/No' Questions

All yes/no questions end in là, which attaches itself to the previous word. The tense particles teh/deh and meh (see page 28) are shortened before là to dhă and mă, creating dhălà and mălà:

Do you want to buy a ticket?	k'ămyà/shin leq-hmaq weh-jin-dhălà? (m/f) (lit: you ticket buy-want-dhălà)
Is he a teacher?	thu s'ăya-là? (lit: he/she teacher-là)

Alternatively, a yes/no question, where you are seeking to confirm a piece of information, can be created by adding **naw** to the end of a statement. This particle is equivalent to phrases like 'isn't it?' and 'don't they?'.

You've got a car, haven't you?	kà shí-deh naw?
	(lit: car have-deh haven't-you?)

You can use **naw** to ask if it's alright to do something.

Can I take your photo?	daq-poun yaiq-meh naw?
	(lit: photo take-meh OK?)

One of the most useful questions is **yá-dhǎlà** (or, more informally **yá-là**). This very versatile phrase can mean among other things 'Is it possible?', 'Is it feasible?', 'Is it permissible?', 'Can I ...?' and 'Do you mind?'.

Is it OK to take photos?	daq-poun yaiq-ló yá-dhǎlà?
	(lit: photo taking yá-dhǎlà?)
Can one go by car?	kà-néh thwà-ló yá-là?
	(lit: car-with going yá-là?)

An affirmative answer is **yá-ba-deh** or **yá-deh** (when spoken fast, **yá-deh** sometimes sounds more like **yá-reh**). If it's not OK, the reply will be **mǎyá-ba-bù** or **mǎyá-bù**.

Information Questions

In English, information questions either begin with 'how' or a 'wh' question word, and all questions have other grammatical complications such as word order changes. In Burmese, there are no changes to word order – all question words begin with b and all information question ends in lèh. As with là, the tense particles teh/deh and meh get shortened to dhă and mă before lèh.

- what   ba   What book do you want?
  ba sa-ouq lo-jin-dhălèh?
  (lit: what book need-want-dhălèh?)

- who   bădhu   Who is this monk?
  di p'où̀n-jì bădhu-lèh?
  (lit: this monk who-lèh?)

- where   beh-hma   Where do you live?
  (at)   k'ămyà/shin beh-hma ne-dhălèh? (m/f)
  (lit: you where live-dhălèh?)

- where   beh-gá   Where have you come from?
  (from)   k'ămyà/shin beh-gá la-dhălèh? (m/f)
  (lit: you which-from come-dhălèh?)

- where   beh-go   Where are you going?
  (to)   k'ămyà/shin beh-go thwà-mălèh? (m/f)
  (lit: you where-to go-mălèh?)

- which   beh   Which car do you like best?
  (noun)   beh kà ăcaiq-s'où̀n-lèh?
  (lit: which car like-'est'-lèh?)

Some question words are more adverbial.

- when   beh-doùn-gá   When were you at school?
  (past)   k'ămyà/shin caùn beh-doùn-
                         gá teq-thălèh? (m/f)
                         (lit: you school when-past
                         attend-thălèh?)

- when   beh-dáw   When will it open?
  (future)   beh-dáw p'wín-mălèh?
                         (lit: when-future open-mălèh?)

- why   ba-p'yiq-ló Why is the bus late?
                         baq-săkà ba-p'yiq-ló
                         nauq-cá-dhălèh?
                         (lit: bus why late-dhălèh?)

- how much beh-lauq   How much is the room?
                         ăk'àn-gá beh-lauq-lèh?
                         (lit: room-charge
                         how-much-lèh?)

- how many beh-hnă   How many people came?
            + counter   lu beh-hnăyauq la-dhălèh?
            (see page 34) (lit: people how-many-persons
                         come-dhălèh?)

(see page 34)

GRAMMAR

Remember, don't change the word order in a question, and there is no need for the pitch of the voice to rise – là or lèh (depending on whether it's a yes/no question or an information question) at the end with a plain high tone is all you need.

ANSWERS

To answer, you can produce a full sentence by repeating everything in the question and providing the necessary new information, but shorter answers are more common and easier.

Answering 'Yes/No' Questions

For a 'yes/no' question, you can simply say:

Yes.	houq-kéh
	or, more politely, houq-pa-deh
	or, to a monk, hman-ba
No.	măhouq-p'ù
	or, more politely, măhouq-pa-bù
	or, to a monk, măhman-ba-bù

Answering Information Questions

To answer an information question, you can either provide the noun or adverb information necessary, or give a full sentence.

What do (you) want?	ba lo-jin-dhălèh?
	(lit: what need-want-dhălèh)
(I want) a ticket.	leq-hmaq (lo-jin-deh)
	(lit: ticket need-want-deh)

Note that 'nothing' is ba-hmá, and 'no-one' is bădhu-hmá. When using either to answer a question, you usually need at least a negated verb (and modals if there are any in the question).

NEGATION

Any sentence can be negated by putting mă- before the verb, and p'ù/bù at the end of the sentence. The verb particle teh/deh is dropped in the negative.

That room is good.	ho ăk'àn kaùn-deh
	(lit: that room good-deh)
That room is not good.	ho ăk'àn măkaùn-bù
	(lit: that room mă-good-bù)

POLITENESS

The Burmese language has a very frequent and important small particle, pa/ba, that makes the whole sentence more polite. It comes after the verb and after the modal if there is one (see page 31 for an explanation of modals), but before any other particles such as those indicating tense. You don't need to put it into every sentence, but try to put it in a few sentences at the start and end of every conversation and make sure you put it into any requests or commands that you make.

Requests or commands do not have a tense particle and, without a politeness particle, will be abrupt.

Please go.	k'ămyà/shin thwà-ba (m/f)
	(lit: you go-ba)
Go!	thwà!

ADVERBS

In Burmese, adverbs can be placed before or after any noun phrase in the sentence, but not normally at the end. Adverbs describing the manner of the verb's action tend to be just before the verb, while sentence adverbs, such as those of time, tend to be closer to the beginning of the sentence.

Yesterday, I arrived at Yangon (Rangoon).
  măné-gá cănaw/cămá yan-goun yauq-teh (m/f)
  (lit: yesterday I Yangon arrive-teh)

Can you come back next year?
  nauq-hniq pyan-la-nain-mălà?
  (lit: next-year return-come-can- mălà?)

This horse runs quickly.
  di myìn myan-myan pyè-deh
  (lit: this horse quick-quick run-deh)

As the last example shows, some adverbs are simply doubled versions of adjective-verbs: myan 'fast', myan-myan 'quickly'; kaùn 'good', kaùn-gaùn 'well'.

GRAMMAR

Some Useful Words

in front	shé	ရှေ့
behind/after (in time)	nauq	နောက်
inside	ăt'èh	အထဲ
outside	ăpyin	အပြင်
between	ăcà/jà	အကြား/ကြား
above/on top of	ăt'eq-/ăpaw	အထက်/အပေါ်
below/under	auq	အောက်
because (beginning of sentence)	ba p'yiq-ló-lèh s'o-dáw	ဘာဖြစ်လို့ လဲဆိုတော့
because (after a verb)	ló	လို့
but	da-be-méh	ဒါပေမဲ့
and (after a noun)	lèh	လည်း
and (after a noun)/with	néh	နဲ့
and then ...	pì-dáw	ပြီးတော့
for (after a noun)	ătweq	အတွက်
every (after a noun)	tàin/dàin	တိုင်း
only (after a noun)	bèh	ပဲ
very	theiq	သိပ်

The grammar in this chapter may seem difficult, but as long as you remember that the verb comes after the noun(s), and that the grammatical particles are put on the end of the word they belong with, you're halfway there. No-one will mind if you make a few mistakes, so go for it!

MEETING PEOPLE

In formal situations and in cities, the first thing you say when meeting someone you don't know is **min-gǎla-ba**, 'It's a blessing'. When you already know someone, a greeting can start by asking about their health. This is no more of a genuine request for a medical report than the English 'How are you?', and is usually answered positively.

YOU SHOULD KNOW သိသင့်သိထိုက်သောအချက်အလက်

Hello. (It's a blessing.)
  min-gǎla-ba   မင်္ဂလာပါ။

Are you well?
  (k'ǎmyà/shin)   (ခင်ဗျာ၊ / ရှင်)
  ne-kaùn-yéh-là? (m/f)   နေကောင်းရဲ့လား။

(I) am well.
  ne-kaùn-ba-deh   နေကောင်းပါတယ်။

What about you?
  k'ǎmyà-yàw/shin-yàw   ခင်ဗျားရော/ ရှင်ရော
  ne-kaùn-yéh-là? (m/f)   နေကောင်းရဲ့လား။

Excuse me. (attracting attention)
  tǎs'eiq-lauq   တစ်ဆိတ်လောက်

Please.
  cè-zù-pyú-bì   ကျေးဇူးပြု၍

Thanks.
  cè-zù naw   ကျေးဇူးနော်။

Thank you.
  cè-zù tin-ba-deh   ကျေးဇူးတင်ပါတယ်။

See you again/later.
  twé-meh naw?   တွေ့ မယ်နော်။
or nauq-twé-dhè-da-báw   နောက်တွေ့ သေးတာပေါ့။

Yes.   houq-kéh   ဟုတ်ကဲ့။
No.   mǎhouq-pa-bù   မဟုတ်ပါဘူး။

GREETINGS & GOODBYES   နှုတ်ဆက်စကား

Greetings may involve asking whether you have eaten, where you are going or where you have come from. The answers to these questions can be quite vague – the questions are not meant to be intrusive.

Have you eaten?
   t'ămìn sà-pì-bi-là?   ထမင်းစားပြီးပြီလား။
I have eaten.
   sà-pì-ba-bi   စားပြီးပါပြီ။

The usual answer, even if you're hungry, is yes, unless, of course, you are arriving at someone's house for dinner!

A common greeting, which you may hear people calling out from the roadside, is:

Where are you going?
   beh thwà-mǎló-lèh?   ဘယ်သွားမလို့ လဲ။

To this, a general, non-specific reply is di-nà-lè-bèh (ဒီနားလေးပဲ), 'Just around here'. If you want to be more specific, however, common replies are:

I am going to the market.
   zè thwà-mǎló   ဈေးသွားမလို့ ။
I am travelling.
   k'ǎyì thwà-mǎló   ခရီးသွားမလို့ ။
I am going to town.
   myó-dèh thwà-mǎló   မြို့ထဲ သွားမလို့ ။

Alternatively, you may be asked if you are going home, or where you have come from:

Are you going home?
    pyan-táw-mălà?   ပြန်တော့မလား။
Where have you been?
    beh-gá la-dhălèh?   ဘယ်က လာသလဲ။

You can be as general or as specific as you wish in your response:

I am going home.
    pyan-táw-meh   ပြန်တော့မယ်။
I am going back to my hotel.
    ho-teh-go pyan-táw-meh   ဟိုတယ်ကို ပြန်တော့မယ်။
I have come from Yangon
(Rangoon).
    yan-goun-gá la-ba-deh   ရန်ကုန်က လာပါတယ်။
I have come from the school/
monastery.
    caùn-gá la-ba-deh   ကျောင်းက လာပါတယ်။
I have come from America.
    ăme-rí-kà-gá la-ba-deh   အမေရိကားက လာပါတယ်။

There is no single phrase for 'goodbye' in Burmese. If someone has helped you, you should first thank them, then say that you were glad to meet them and that you are going. Finally, you can say that you will see them later. As in English, this does not necessarily imply a commitment to see them again. The phrases used can also depend on whether you are leaving or being left behind.

Thank you very much!
    ămyà-jì cè-zù tin-ba-deh   အများကြီး ကျေးဇူးတင်ပါတယ်။
I'm glad to meet you.
    k'ămyà/shin-néh twé-ya-da   ခင်ဗျာ/ရှင်နဲ့
    wùn-tha-ba-deh (m/f)   တွေ့ရတာ ဝမ်းသာပါတယ်။

I enjoyed talking to you.
    săga-pyàw-ló kaùn-ba-deh   စကားပြောလို့ ကောင်းပါတယ်။

Are you going home?
    pyan-táw-mălà?   ပြန်တော့မလား။

Are you leaving now?
    thwà-táw-mălà?   သွားတော့မလား။

I'm leaving now.
    thwà-ba-oùn-meh   သွားပါအုံးမယ်။

I'm leaving, OK?
    thwà-meh naw?   သွားမယ်နော်။

I'm going home, OK?
    pyan-meh naw?   ပြန်မယ်နော်။

Please don't go!
    măthwà-ba-néh-oùn!   မသွားပါနဲ့ အုံး။

OK, go. (goodbye)
    kaùn-ba-bi   ကောင်းပါပြီ။

Take it easy.
    pyè-byè (lit: go slowly)   ဖြည်းဖြည်း

See you again/later.
    twé-meh, naw?   တွေ့ မယ်နော်။
    or nauq-twé-dhè-da-báw   နောက်တွေ့ သေးတာပေါ့။

HEY YOU!

As you walk around, you'll hear young people shouting out 'Hey you!' or 'Peace!' (the latter often sounds more like 'piss'). They find this particularly amusing since in Burmese yù (ရူး) means 'mad' or 'insane'. This could be your first introduction to the Burmese love of punning. You can give as good as you get by replying măyù-ba-bù (မရူးပါဘူး), 'I'm not crazy'.

CIVILITIES
ယဉ်ကျေးဖွယ်ရာစကား

A smile is often enough to express gratitude when someone is
doing their job or a small favour – thanking tends to be reserved
for larger favours. However, as more people in Myanmar meet
foreigners, saying 'thank you' is becoming more common:

Thanks.
    cè-zù naw   ကျေးဇူးနော်။
Thank you.
    cè-zù tin-ba-deh   ကျေးဇူးတင်ပါတယ်။

The response may be:

It's nothing. (you're welcome)
    keiq-sá măshí-ba-bù   ကိစ္စမရှိပါဘူး။

If you think something you want is a favour, you could use cè-zù
pyú-bi, 'having thanked you', before the request. This makes it even
more polite than just pa/ba at the end (see Grammar, page 39).

Please help.
    cè-zù pyú-bì ku-nyi-ba   ကျေးဇူးပြုပြီး ကူညီပါ။

Unlike in English, expressing sorrow or sympathy frequently with
people you don't know is not widespread. You don't need to say
'sorry' every time you brush someone in the street or to attract
someone's attention. However, if you want to apologise for
doing something to someone, eg, treading on their toe, or for
not doing something, eg, not giving alms, it's:

I'm sorry/I apologise.
    taùn-ban-ba-deh   တောင်းပန်ပါတယ်။
Please excuse me.
    gădáw-ba-deh   ကန်တော့ပါတယ်။

To express regret, use:

(I) am sorry.
    wùn-nèh-ba-deh   ဝမ်းနဲပါတယ်။

To express pleasure or congratulate someone, you can say:

(I) am glad.
    wùn-tha-ba-deh   ဝမ်းသာပါတယ်။

You can use these phrases in longer sentences too:

(I) am very sorry that (your) father died.
    ăp'e s'oùn-thwà-da   အဖေဆုံးသွားတာ
    theiq wùn-nèh-ba-deh   သိပ်ဝမ်းနဲ့ပါတယ်။

One frequent phrase is:

Don't feel bad about it./Don't be embarrassed.
    à-măna-ba-néh   အားမနာပါနဲ့။

People generally say this when they want to give you something or do something for you, and don't want you to refuse. However, sometimes they will say it even if they hope you will refuse. If someone says this to you and you accept, you should respond by thanking them. If you want to decline the offer, or to be polite, you might reply:

I do feel bad about it.
    à-na-ba-deh   အားနာပါတယ်။

TALKING TO MONKS ဘုန်းကြီးနှင့်စကားပြောခြင်း

When speaking to monks, you should try to use a special honorific vocabulary. This covers both common pronouns and phrases, and also everyday actions, like eating and sleeping, when carried out by a monk. Women should avoid touching monks or their clothes, or even approaching too close and should not hand items directly to monks but should place them in front of them or give them to a lay assistant.

I (layperson)
  dăbyí-daw/
  dăbyí-daw-má (m/f)   တပည့်တော်/ တပည့်တော်မ
I (monk)
  p'oùn-jì/ù-băzìn   ဘုန်းကြီး/ ဦးပဉ္စင်း
you (to senior monk)
  s'ăya-daw   ဆရာတော်
you (to a monk)
  ăshin-păyà/ù-băzìn   အရှင်ဘုရား/ ဦးပဉ္စင်း
you (to a novice)
  ko-yin   ကိုရင်
you (monk to layperson)
  dăgà/dăgà-má (m/f)   ဒကာ/ ဒကာမ

Yes. (as in 'I follow you.')
  tin-ba   တင်ပါ
Yes. (as in 'That's true.')
  hman-ba   မှန်ပါ

The layperson phrase for 'I' (dăbyí-daw/dăbyí-daw-má, တပည့်တော်/ တပည့်တော်မ) literally means 'revered pupil' or 'follower'.

Nuns do not receive the same special treatment, but you should call them s'ăya-lè (ဆရာလေး), 'little master'.

If you remember to use any of these phrases when speaking to a monk, you will greatly impress your Burmese friends as a thoroughly cultivated individual.

MEETING PEOPLE

FORMS OF ADDRESS   အခေါ်အဝေါ်အသုံးအနှုန်း

Burmese people usually have two-word names (sometimes more; infrequently only one). There is no family name, no change of name on marriage and no abbreviation, except among close friends and family. One of a variety of titles may be placed before this name, like English 'Mr', but these titles are used according to age, prestige and level of intimacy – not marital status.

	for men		for women	
to someone older/respected	ù	ဦး	daw	ဒေါ်
to someone of the same age	ko	ကို	mámá/daw	မမ/ဒေါ်
to someone younger/intimate	maun(g)	မောင်	má	မ

Use of a name without one of these titles is also possible among close friends. A man named Soe Win, for example, could be called U Soe Win, Ko Soe Win or even Ko Soe, Maun(g) Soe Win or just Soe Win; a lady named Khin Than could be called Daw Khin Than or Ma Khin Than (using just Khin Than, Khin or Than alone would imply quite close friendship).

Sometimes an occupational title is used instead of, or before, another title:

General Aung San
   bo-jouq aun s'àn   ဗိုလ်ချုပ်အောင်ဆန်း
Teacher U Hla Han
   s'ǎya ù hlá han   ဆရာ ဦးလှဟန်
Teacher Daw Khin Khin Myint
   s'ǎya-ma daw k'in k'in myín   ဆရာမ ဒေါ်ခင်ခင်မြင့်
Doctor Ba U (m)
   dauq-ta bá ù   ဒေါက်တာ ဘဦး

The polite way to attract someone's attention is to say the pronoun form 'you': **k'ǎmyà** (ခင်ဗျား), if you are a man; and **shin** (ရှင်), if you are a woman (see Grammar, page 26). If the person you wish to talk with has an obvious title, you should use that instead, eg, 'teacher', **s'ǎya/s'ǎya-má** (m/f) (ဆရာ/ဆရာမ); 'military officer (captain)', **bo-jì** (ဗိုလ်ကြီး); 'general', **bo-jouq** (ဗိုလ်ချုပ်) and so on. For monks there is a special honorific vocabulary (see Talking to Monks, page 47).

You may also tack 'you' or any kind of title onto the end of anything you say, to make a request or statement even more polite:

Please come, sir.
   la-ba k'ǎmyà/shin (m/f)   လာပါ ခင်ဗျား/ရှင်။
Good, teacher.
   kaùn-ba-deh s'ǎya   ကောင်းပါတယ် ဆရာ။
Yes. (to a monk)
   hman-ba p'ǎyà   မှန်ပါ ဘုရား။
   (lit: correct Buddha)

NAMING NAMES

The day of the week on which a person is born determines the letter with which their name begins:

Sunday	vowels
Monday	k, k', g, ng
Tuesday	s, s', z, ny
Wednesday	
morning	l, w
afternoon	y
Thursday	p, p', b, m
Friday	th, h
Saturday	t, t', d, n

For example, we know that U Nu, **ù nú** (ဦးနု), would have been born on a Saturday. If you are given a name, make sure it begins with the right letter.

MEETING PEOPLE

MEETING PEOPLE

WHAT'S IN A NAME?

Burmese names all have a meaning. They can be determined by the day of the week a person is born, the position of the child in the family, the advice of a fortune-teller or monk, his or her parent's own name, or the attributes the parents would like to see the child acquire, such as success or good health. Below are some common Burmese names and their meanings:

SUNDAY

Arnt	án	အံ့	wondrous
Aung	aun	အောင်	successful
Aye	è	အေး	cool, placid
Ohnmar	oun-ma	ဥမ္မာ	a woman so beautiful she drove men mad
Oo/U	ù	ဦး	first

MONDAY

Khin	k'in	ခင်	friendly
Ko	ko	ကို	brother
Kyaw	caw	ကျော်	famous
Kyi	ci	ကြည်	clear
Kyi/Gyi	cì/jì	ကြီး	big
Kyine/Kyaing	cain	ကြိုင်	fragrant
Kyaw/Gyaw	c'àw/jàw	ချော	handsome

TUESDAY

Nyi	nyi	ညီ	little brother
Sabeh/Sabai	săbeh	စံပယ်	jasmine
San	s'àn	ဆန်း	extraordinary
Sanda	san-da	စန္ဒာ	moon
Sein	sein	စိန်	diamond
Soe/So	sò	စိုး	dominate
Zaw	zàw	ဇော	ardent

WEDNESDAY

morning

Lay	lè	လေး	little
Lin	lìn	လင်း	bright
Lwin	lwin	လွင်	distinct
We	we	ဝေ	luxuriant

afternoon

Yi	yì	ရယ်	laughing
Yin	yin	ယဉ်	cultured, gentle
Ye	yèh	ရဲ	brave

THURSDAY

Hpyo/Pyo	p'yò	ဖြိုး	prosperous
Mar	ma	မာ	healthy
Moe	mò	မိုး	rain, sky
Mya	myá	မြ	emerald
Myat	myaq	မြတ်	noble

FRIDAY

Thanda	than-da	သန္တာ	coral
Thawda/Thawdar	thaw-da	သော်တာ	moon
Thazin	thăzin	သဇင်	orchid
Thein	theìn	သေမာ	forest
Theingi/Thanegi	thein-gi	သီဂိ	gold
Thuza	thu-za	သုဇာ	heavenly queen

SATURDAY

Ne/Nay	ne	နေ	sun
Nilar	ni-la	နီလာ	sapphire
Nu	nú	နု	soft, youthful
Nwe	nwéh	နွဲ့	graceful
Tu	t'ù	ထူး	special

BEHAVIOUR   အမူအရာ

When greeting people, some Burmese men may shake hands, particularly if they are used to Western practices. Women may simply nod, or perform a Thai 'wai' with two hands together in a prayer position. Hugging and kissing is not usual, and bodily contact in public is generally frowned upon, although holding hands between sexes is common, and if you are a woman, you may find a Burmese girl taking your hand to show you something. Burmese women rarely go anywhere on their own and, if you are travelling alone as a woman, you may find they insist on accompanying you.

To hand small objects to others, such as visiting cards, you should use your right hand and, as a sign of particular care and respect, touch your left hand on your right wrist as you do so. Both hands should be used for large objects. Beckoning with the hand should be done with the fingers pointed downwards.

Feet are regarded as unclean, and when sitting, avoid pointing your feet at other people, particularly monks. You should also avoid turning your back on pagodas and Buddha statues.

SHOWING RESPECT

If you are speaking to someone who you barely know, and you don't feel comfortable calling them 'Auntie' or 'Uncle' (see Grammar, page 27), then calling them s'ăya (m) or s'ăya-má (f) is often an easy way out – as well as flattering the person you are speaking to. It not only means 'teacher' in the academic sense, but any skilled practitioner, from whom you could potentially learn something, such as a doctor, a writer, an artist or even the driver of your car or bus. Servants and junior staff usually call their bosses s'ăya or s'ăya-má just to be on the safe side.

MEETING PEOPLE

You should not touch or pat people on the head. If you are walking in front of someone who is seated, particularly if they are older, you should bow your head and shoulders slightly as you pass.

Women should avoid placing themselves or their clothing above men, for example by sitting on the roof of transport, as this diminishes their **p'oùn** (ဘုန်း), 'masculinity'. Similarly, women hanging their clothes out to dry should ensure they are not above or touching those of the men.

Gesticulating while speaking is not particularly common, but it can be helpful to make a point. To show assent, Burmese people usually nod, as in the West, and to show they are following you, may repeatedly remark **houq-kéh** (ဟုတ်ကဲ့), meaning 'Yes' or 'It is true'. Smiling is always a good strategy. As in most Asian cultures, losing one's temper and shouting is rarely productive and leads to loss of face on both sides.

FIRST ENCOUNTERS

ပထမအကြိမ်တွေ့ဆုံခြင်း

What is your name?
   k'ămyá/shín na-meh
   beh-lo k'aw-dhălèh? (m/f)

ခင်ဗျာ/ရှင် နာမည်
ဘယ်လို ခေါ်သလဲ။

My name is ...
   (**cănaw/cămá**) ... **ló**
   k'aw-ba-deh (m/f)

(ကျွန်တော်/ကျွန်မ) ... လို့
ခေါ်ပါတယ်။

I'd like to introduce you to ...
   ... **néh meiq-s'eq-pè-jin-ba-deh**

... နဲ့ မိတ်ဆက်ပေးချင်ပါတယ်။

Pleased to meet you.
   twé-yá-da wùn-tha-ba-deh

တွေ့ရတာ ဝမ်းသာပါတယ်။

MEETING PEOPLE

MAKING CONVERSATION   စကားလက်ဆက်ကျခြင်း

Burmese people are very hospitable and also very inquisitive.
You will readily be invited into homes and offered tea and
snacks, but you will also be subject to questions about your
marital status, children and salary. Other topics that you might
often discuss, such as the weather, are less frequently discussed
in Myanmar.

We're friends.
  dó thăngeh-jìn-dwe-ba   ဒို့သူငယ်ချင်းတွေပါ။
It's very hot, isn't it!
  theiq pu-deh naw?   သိပ်ပူတယ်နော်။
Do you live near here?
  di-nà-hma ne-dhălà?   ဒီနားမှာနေသလား။
Can I take a photo (of you)?
  (k'ămyà-go/shin-go) daq-poun   (ခင်ဗျားကို/ရှင်ကို)
  yaiq-nain-mălà? (m/f)   ဓာတ်ပုံရိုက်နိုင်မလား။
We'll send you one.
  tăk'ú pó-pè-meh   တစ်ခုပို့ပေးမယ်။
What's this called?
  da-go beh-lo-k'aw-lèh?   ဒါကိုဘယ်လိုခေါ်လဲ။
Are you here on holiday?
  ăleh la-da-là?   အလည်လာတာလား။

I'm here ...	... la-ba-deh	... လာပါတယ်။
for a holiday	ăleh	အလည်
on business	sì-bwà-yè-néh	စီးပွားရေးနဲ့
for work	ălouq-ătweq	အလုပ်အတွက်
to study	lé-la-bó-ătweq	လေ့လာဖို့အတွက်

How long are you here for?
    beh-lauq ca-ja   ဘယ်လောက်ကြာကြာနေမလဲ။
    ne-mălèh?

I'm here for ... days.
    cănaw/cămá di-hma ...   ကျွန်တော်/ ကျွန်မ
    yeq ne-meh (m/f)   ဒီမှာ ... ရက်နေမယ်။

We're here for ... weeks.
    cănaw-dó/cămá-dó di-hma   ကျွန်တော်တို့/ ကျွန်မတို့ ဒီမှာ
    ... paq ne-já-meh (m/f)   ... ပတ်နေကြမယ်။

Do you like it here?
    di-hma pyaw-là?   ဒီမှာ ပျော်လား။

We like it here./We're very
happy here.
    di-hma ăyàn-pyaw-ne-deh   ဒီမှာအရမ်းနေတယ်။

Just a minute.
    k'ăná-lè naw   ခဏလေး နော်။

This is my address.
    da cănáw/cămá   ဒါ ကျွန်တော်/
    leiq-sa-ba (m/f)   ကျွန်မ လိပ်စာပါ။

Really!
    houq-là!   ဟုတ်လား

You're right.
    hman-ba-deh   မှန်ပါတယ်။

I don't think so.
    măt'in-bù   မထင်ဘူး။

address
    leiq-sa   လိပ်စာ

close/childhood friend
    thăngeh-jìn   သူငယ်ချင်း

friend
    meiq-s'we   မိတ်ဆွေ

NATIONALITIES   လူမျိုးများ

Where do you live?
k'ămyà/shin beh-hma   ခင်ဗျား/ ရှင်
ne-dhălèh? (m/f)   ဘယ်မှာနေသလဲ။

What is your nationality?
k'ămyà/shin   ခင်ဗျား/ ရှင်
ba-lu-myò-lèh? (m/f)   ဘာလူမျိုးလဲ။

You can ask this question to find out about ethnicity (Shan, Chin etc). Minorities are listed on page 125.

I am ...	cănaw/cămá ...	ကျွန်တော်/ ကျွန်မ ...
	lu-myò-ba (m/f)	လူမျိုးပါ။
Chinese	tăyouq	တရုတ်
French	pyin-thiq	ပြင်သစ်
Sri Lankan	thi-ho	သီဟိုဠ်
Thai	yò-dăyà/t'aìn	ယိုးဒယား/ ထိုင်း

For all other nationalities, just say the words in English – providing the person has heard of the country, they'll recognise it.

I live in/at the/a ...	... hma ne-ba-deh	... မှာ နေပါတယ်။
city	myó	မြို့
countryside	neh	နယ်
mountains	taun-baw	တောင်ပေါ်
seaside	pin-leh-nà-hma	ပင်လယ်နား မှာ
suburbs of ...	... s'in-je-boùn	... ဆင်ခြေဖုံး
village	ywa	ရွာ

CULTURAL DIFFERENCES   ယဉ်ကျေးမှုကွဲခြားချက်များ

How do you do this in
your country?

   k'ămyà-dó nain-ngan-hma   ခင်ဗျားတို့ နိုင်ငံမှာ ဒီဟာကို
   di-ha-go beh-lo louq-thălèh? (m)   ဘယ်လို လုပ်သလဲ။

I don't want to offend you.

   k'ămyà-go/shin-go seiq   ခင်ဗျားကို/ရှင့်ကို ခင်ဗျား
   ănauq-ăsheq   စိတ်အနှောင့်အယှက်
   mǎp'yiq-se-jin-ba-bù (m/f)   မဖြစ်စေချင်ပါဘူး။

I'm sorry, it's not the custom
in my country.

   seiq mǎshí-ba-néh,   စိတ်မရှိပါနဲ့၊ ကျွန်တော်တို့
   cǎnaw-dó   နိုင်ငံရဲ့ဓလေ့
   nain-ngan-yéh dǎ-lé   မဟုတ်လို့ပါ။
   mǎhouq-ló-ba (m)

I'm sorry, it's	seiq mǎshí-ba-néh,	စိတ်မရှိပါနဲ့၊
against my ...	cǎnáw/cǎmá ... (m/f)	ကျွန်တော့်/ကျွန်မ ...
	néh s'án-jin-ne-ló-ba	နဲ့ ဆန့်ကျင်နေလို့ပါ။
beliefs	youn-ci-hmú	ယုံကြည်မှု
culture	yin-jè-hmú	ယဉ်ကျေးမှု
religion	ba-tha-yè	ဘာသာရေး

I don't mind watching, but I'd
prefer not to participate.

   cí-yá-youn-gá-dáw-   ကြည့်ရရင်ကတော့အကြောင်း
   ăcaùn mǎhouq-ba-bù,   မဟုတ်ပါဘူး၊
   da-be-méh theiq-táw   ဒါပေမဲ့ သိပ်တော့
   mǎlouq-c'in-ba-bù   မလုပ်ချင်ပါဘူး။

I'll give it a go.

   sàn-cí-meh   စမ်းကြည့်မယ်။

AGE အသက်အရွယ်

Age is respected in Myanmar, so younger people listen when their elders are speaking.

How old are you?
: **k'ămyà/shin ătheq beh-lauq shí-bi-lèh?** (m/f) — ခင်ဗျား/ရှင် အသက် ဘယ်လောက်ရှိပြီလဲ။

I am ... years old.
: **cănaw/cămá (ătheq) ... hniq shí-bi** (m/f) — ကျွန်တော်/ကျွန်မ (အသက်) ... နှစ် ရှိပြီ။

See the Numbers & Amounts chapter, page 153, for numbers.

OCCUPATIONS အလုပ်အကိုင်များ

What is your occupation?
: **k'ămyà/shin ba ălouq louq-dhălèh?** (m/f) — ခင်ဗျား/ရှင် ဘာအလုပ်လုပ်သလဲ။

I am a/an ...	**cănaw/cămá ... ba** (m/f)	ကျွန်တော်/ကျွန်မ ... ပါ။
accountant	**săyìn-kain**	စာရင်းကိုင်
artist	**păji-s'ăya**	ပန်းချီဆရာ
businessperson	**sì-bwà-yè-dhămà**	စီးပွားရေးသမား
clerk	**săyè**	စာရေး
dentist	**thwà-s'ăya-wun**	သွားဆရာဝန်
diplomat	**than-tăman**	သံတမန်
doctor	**s'ăya-wun**	ဆရာဝန်
engineer	**seq-hmú-pyin-nya-s'ăya**	စက်မှုပညာဆရာ
	in-jin-ni-ya	အင်ဂျင်နီယာ
farmer	**leh-dhămà**	လယ်သမား
government worker	**ăhmú-dàn/ ăya-shí/ ăsò-yá wun-dàn**	အမှုထမ်း/ အရာရှိ/ အစိုးရ ဝန်ထမ်း
journalist	**dhădìn-za-s'ăya**	သတင်းစာဆရာ
lawyer	**shé-ne**	ရှေ့နေ
nurse	**thu-na-byú**	သူနာပြု

photographer	daq-poun-s'ăya	ဓါတ်ပုံဆရာ
researcher	thú-te-thi	သုတေသီ
scientist	theiq-pan-pyin-nya-shin	သိပ္ပံပညာရှင်
soldier	siq-thà	စစ်သား
student	caùn-dhà/ caùn-thu (m/f)	ကျောင်းသား/ ကျောင်းသူ
teacher	caùn-s'ăya caùn-s'ăya-má (m/f)	ကျောင်းဆရာ ကျောင်းဆရာမ
university lecturer	tek-kădho kăt'í-ká	တက္ကသိုလ်ကထိက
waiter	săbwèh-dò	စားပွဲထိုး
writer	sa-yè-s'ăya	စာရေးဆရာ

Some other typically Burmese occupations are:

actor	thăyouq-s'aun	သရုပ်ဆောင်
agent/broker	pwèh-sà	ပွဲစား
driver	kà-maùn-thămà	ကားမောင်းသမား
fortune-teller	be-din-s'ăya	ဗေဒင်ဆရာ
guide	gaiq/làn-hnyun	ဂိုက်/လမ်းညွှန်
market seller	zè-theh	ဈေးသည်
merchant/trader	koun-theh	ကုန်သည်
monk	p'oùn-gyì	ဘုန်းကြီး
nat medium (male)	naq-s'ăya	နတ်ဆရာ
nat medium (female)	naq-gădaw	နတ်ကတော်
rickshaw-driver	s'aiq-kà-dhămà	ဆိုက်ကားသမား
sailor	thìn-bàw-dhà	သင်္ဘောသား
shop-owner	s'ain-pain-shin	ဆိုင်ပိုင်ရှင်
singer	ăs'o-daw	အဆိုတော်

I'm retired.
　　cănaw/cămá ănyeìn-zà-ba (m/f) 　ကျွန်တော်/ကျွန်မ အငြိမ်းစားပါ။
I'm unemployed.
　　cănaw/cămá ălouq 　　　　　　ကျွန်တော်/ကျွန်မ
　　măshí-bù (m/f) 　　　　　　　　အလုပ်မရှိဘူး။

RELIGION ဘာသာရေး

What is your religion?
k'ămyà/shin beh-ba-dha gweh-dhălèh? (m/f) ခင်ဗျား/ရှင် ဘယ်ဘာသာ ကိုးကွယ်သလဲ။

I am ... **cănaw/cămá ... ba (m/f)** ကျွန်တော်/ကျွန်မ ... ပါ။

Buddhist	**bouq-dá ba-dha**	ဗုဒ္ဓ ဘာသာ
Christian	**k'ăriq-yan**	ခရစ်ယာန်
Hindu	**hein-du ba-dha**	ဟိန္ဒူ ဘာသာ
Jewish	**gyù ba-dha**	ဂျူး ဘာသာ
Muslim	**muq-sălin ba-dha**	မွတ်စလင်ဘာသာ

I am not religious.
ba ba-dha-hmá măkò-gweh-bù ဘာဘာသာမှ မကိုးကွယ်ဘူး။

I am interested in Buddhism.
bouq-dá ba-dha seiq-win-sà-ba-deh ဗုဒ္ဓဘာသာ စိတ်ဝင်စားပါတယ်။

Can I attend this service?
di wuq-pyú-s'ú-daùn-bwèh-go teq-ló yá-mălà? ဒီဝတ်ပြုဆုတောင်းပွဲကို တက်လို့ ရမလား။

Is this service in English?
di wuq-pyú s'ú-daùn-bwèh-gá ìn-găleiq-lo-là? ဒီဝတ်ပြုဆုတောင်းပွဲက အင်္ဂလိပ်လိုလား။

Am I allowed to enter the temple?
p'ăyà-dèh-go win-k'wín yá-mălà? ဘုရားထဲကို ဝင်ခွင့်ရမလား။

How many monks are there in the monastery?
di-jaùn-hma than-ga beh-hnăpà shí-lèh? ဒီကျောင်းမှာ သံဃာဘယ်နှစ်ပါး ရှိလဲ။

I'd like to meet the abbot.
s'ăya-daw-néh twé-jin-ba-deh ဆရာတော်နဲ့ တွေ့ချင်ပါတယ်။

church	p'ăyà shiq-k'o-jaùn	ဘုရားရှိခိုးကျောင်း
funeral	ăthú-bá	အသုဘ
God	p'ăyà thăk'in	ဘုရားသခင်
lay assistant	kaq-pí-yá	ကပ္ပိယ
pagoda trustees	gàw-păká ăp'wéh	ဂေါပကအဖွဲ့
prayer	wuq-p'yu-hmú	ဝတ်ပြုမှု
procession	shin-byú hléh-leh-da	ရှင်ပြုလှည့်လည်တာ
relic	daq-taw	ဓာတ်တော်
shrine (Buddha)	p'ăyà-zin	ဘုရားစင်
shrine (nat)	naq-sin	နတ်စင်

BUDDHISM

ဗုဒ္ဓဘာသာ

abbot (head of monastery)	săya-daw	ဆရာတော်
authority	àw-za	ဩဇာ
Bodhisattiva (future Buddha)	p'ăyà-laùn	ဘုရားလောင်း
Buddhism	bouq-dá ba-dha	ဗုဒ္ဓဘာသာ
footprint of Buddha	c'e-daw-ya	ခြေတော်ရာ
good deed	kaùn-hmú	ကောင်းမှု
ordination hall	thein	သိမ်
initiate a novice	shin-pyú-deh	ရှင်ပြုတယ်
karma/fate	kan	ကံ
merit	kú-tho	ကုသိုလ်
monastery/temple	p'oùn-jì-jaùn	ဘုန်းကြီးကျောင်း
pagoda trustee	p'ăyà-lu-jì	ဘုရားလူကြီး
monk (over 20)	p'oùn-jì	ဘုန်းကြီး
nirvana/enlightenment	neiq-ban	နိဗ္ဗာန်
novice (young man)	shin/ko-yin	ရှင်/ကိုရင်
nun	thi-lá-shin	သီလရှင်
power/authority (male)	p'oùn	ဘုန်း
rest house	zăyaq	ဇရပ်
stairway (up to a temple)	zaùn-dàn	စောင်းတန်း
stupa/chedi	ze-di	စေတီ
virtue/prestige	goun	ဂုဏ်

PERSON CROSSING

One of the best ways of getting to know Burmese people is to act as a **lu-joun** (လူကြူ), literally 'person crossing', by delivering lettter or photos from Burmese relatives abroad or other travellers. The postal system is very unreliable, so hand delivery is more secure. In addition to letters and photos, it is worth carrying a few magazines to give away.

INTERESTS & ACTIVITIES

ဝါသနာများ

What sport do you play?
ba à-găzà louq-thălèh? ဘာ အားကစား လုပ်သလဲ။

Do you like sport?	à-găzà caiq-thălà?	အားကစားကြိုက်သလား။
Yes, very much.	theiq caiq-ba-deh	သိပ်ကြိုက်ပါတယ်။
No, not at all.	loùn-wá măcaiq-bù	လုံးဝ မကြိုက်ဘူး။
I like watching it.	cí-yá-da caiq-teh	ကြည့်ရတာ ကြိုက်တယ်။

What do you do in your free time?
ăc'ein-à-yin ba-louq-lé-shí-lèh? အချိန်အားရင် ဘာလုပ်လေ့ရှိလဲ။

I play/practise ...	... găzà-deh	... ကစားတယ်။
aerobics	è-rò-biq	အေရိုဗစ်
archery	lè-ătaq	လေးအတတ်
athletics	pyè-k'oun-pyiq (lit: run-jump-throw)	ပြေးခုန်ပစ်
baseball	bé-săbàw	ဘေ့စဘော
basketball	baq-săkeq-bàw	ဘတ်စကက်ဘော
boxing	leq-hwé	လက်ဝှေ့
cricket	k'riq-keq	ခရစ်ကက်
fencing	dà-gouq	ဓားခုတ်
football (soccer)	bàw-loùn	ဘောလုံး
gymnastics	cùn-bà	ကျွမ်းဘား
hockey (field)	haw-ki	ဟော်ကီ
judo	ju-do	ဂျူဒို
martial arts	thàin	သိုင်း
rugby	raq-găbi-bàw-loùn	ရတ်ဂဘီဘောလုံး
table tennis	zăbwèh-din tìn-niq	စားပွဲတင်တင်းနစ်
tennis	tìn-niq	တင်းနစ်
volleyball	baw-li-bàw	ဘော်လီဘော

MEETING PEOPLE

I play badminton.	ceq-taun yaiq-teh	ကြက်တောင်ရိုက်တယ်။
I climb.	taun teq-teh	တောင်တက်တယ်။
I cycle.	seq-beìn sì-deh	စက်ဘီးစီးတယ်။
I dance.	ká-taq-teh	ကတတ်တယ်။
I play golf.	gauf yaiq-teh	ဂေါဖ်ရိုက်တယ်။
I go hiking.	c'e-lyin k'ăyì t'weq-teh	ခြေလျင်ခရီးထွက်တယ်။
I ice skate.	ye-gèh-byin-dwin skeiq-sì-deh	ရေခဲပြင်တွင် စကိတ်စီးတယ်။
I jog.	ămyan-làn shauq-teh	အမြန်လမ်းလျှောက်တယ်။
I horse ride.	myìn sì-deh	မြင်းစီးတယ်။
I row.	hle hlaw-deh	လှေလှော်တယ်။
I sail.	yweq taiq-teh	ရွက်တိုက်တယ်။
I scuba dive.	le-ò-byín ye-ngouq-teh	လေအိုးဖြင့်ရေငုပ်တယ်။

I shoot.	thănaq pyiq-teh	သေနတ်ပစ်တယ်။
I (downhill) ski.	hnìn-gèh-byin shàw-sì-deh	နှင်းခဲပြင် လျှောစီးတယ်။
I snorkel.	le-bun-byín ye-ngouq-teh	လေပြွန်ဖြင့်ရေငုပ်တယ်။
I play squash.	sqwaq yaiq-deh	စကွပ်ရိုက်တယ်။
I surf.	ye-hlaìn-sì-deh	ရေလှိုင်းစီးတယ်။
I swim.	ye kù-deh	ရေကူးတယ်။
I water-ski.	ye-hlwa-shàw-sì-deh	ရေလွှာလျှောစီးတယ်။
I lift weights.	ălè má-deh	အလေးမတယ်။
I windsurf.	le-hlaìn-sì-deh	လေလှိုင်းစီးတယ်။
I wrestle.	năbàn loùn-deh	နပန်းလုံးတယ်။

I like ...	... wa-thăna pa-deh	... ဝါသနာပါတယ်။
birdwatching	cè-ngeq	ကျေးငှက်
	cí-shú-lé-la-da	ကြည့်ရှုလေလာတာ
cooking	hìn-ceq-ta	ဟင်းချက်တာ
drawing	poun-s'wèh-da	ပုံဆွဲတာ
eating out	ăpyin-t'weq-sà-da	အပြင်ထွက်စားတာ
knitting	thò-hmwè-t'ò-da	သိုးမွေးထိုးတာ
listening	tè-thăjìn nà-t'aun-da	တေးသီချင်း
to music		နားထောင်တာ
meditation	tăyà-t'ain-da	တရားထိုင်တာ
painting	păjì-s'wèh-da	ပန်းချီဆွဲတာ
photography	daq-poun-yaiq-ta	ဓါတ်ပုံရိုက်တာ
playing cards	p'èh-găzà-da	ဖဲကစားတာ
playing music	tè-thăjìn tì-da	တေးသီချင်းတီးတာ
reading	sa p'aq-ta	စာဖတ်တာ
watching films	youq-shin cí-da	ရုပ်ရှင် ကြည့်တာ
yoga	yàw-gá ăcín	ယောဂအကျင့်

FAMILY

မိသားစု

Although asking about someone's marital status is quite common, asking someone if they have a boyfriend or girlfriend is regarded as a very personal question, to be avoided.

Are you married?
k'ămyà/shin ein-daun
shí-dhălà? (m/f)

ခင်ဗျား/ရှင်
အိမ်ထောင်ရှိသလား။

I am /You are married.
ein-daun shí-ba-deh

အိမ်ထောင်ရှိပါတယ်။

I am not married.
cănaw/cămá ein-daun
măshí-ba-bù (m/f)

ကျွန်တော်/ကျွန်မ
အိမ်ထောင်မရှိပါဘူး။

How many brothers and sisters do you have?
maun-hnămá beh-hnăyauq shí-dhălèh? — မောင်နှမ ဘယ်နှယောက် ရှိသလဲ။

How old are they?
thu-dó ătheq beh-lauq-shí-dhălèh? — သူတို့အသက်ဘယ်လောက်ရှိသလဲ။

How many children do you have?
kălè beh-hnăyauq shí-dhălèh? — ကလေးဘယ်နှစ်ယောက်ရှိသလဲ။

Do you have (a/an) ...?	**... shí-dhălà?**	... ရှိသလား။
I have (a/an) ...	**(cănaw/cămá) ... shí-ba-deh** (m/f)	(ကျွန်တော်/ကျွန်မ) ... ရှိပါတယ်။
I have no ...	**(cănaw/cămá) ... măshí-ba-bù** (m/f)	(ကျွန်တော်/ကျွန်မ) ... မရှိပါဘူး။
baby	**kălè-ngeh**	ကလေးငယ်
children	**thà-dhămì**	သားသမီး
daughter	**thămì**	သမီး
family	**mí-thà-sú**	မိသားစု
father	**ăp'e**	အဖေ
grandfather	**ăp'ò**	အဘိုး
grandmother	**ăp'wà**	အဘွား
husband/man	**yauq-cà**	ယောကျ်ား
mother	**ăme**	အမေ
older brother	**ăko**	အစ်ကို
younger brother	**nyi/maun** (of male/of female)	ညီ/မောင်
older sister	**ămá**	အစ်မ
younger sister	**hnămá/nyi-má** (of male/of female)	နှမ/ညီမ
son	**thà**	သား
wife (less polite)	**meìn-má**	မိန်းမ
wife (more polite)	**zănì**	ဇနီး

POLITICS နိုင်ငံရေး

This is a sensitive topic. You should tread very carefully. You will see large billboards with current slogans in front of many government offices; most of these are fairly general and unexceptionable: ' Love and cherish the motherland' or similar.

democracy	di-mo-kăre-si	ဒီမိုကရေစီ
election	ywè-kauq-pwèh	ရွေ:ကောက်ပွဲ
government	ăsò-yá	အစိုးရ
military intelligence	t'auq-hlàn-yè/M.I.	ထောက်လှမ်:ရေ:/ အမ်အိုင်
political party	pa-ti	ပါတီ
politics	nain-ngan-yè	နိုင်ငံရေး
prison	ăcìn-daun	အကျဉ်:ထောင်

The military government, which took over in late 1988, was previously known as the State Law and Order Restoration Council or SLORC (ná-wá-tá, န၀တ). It changed its name in 1997 to State Peace and Development Council (SPDC or ná-yá-ká, နရက). The Union Solidarity and Development Association (USDA or pye-k'ain-p'yò, ပြည်နိုင်ငံဖွံ့.) was established as a government-run civilian organisation in 1993 and has branches throughout the country recognised by the red, green and yellow signboards with a chinthe, 'lion'. Non-members call it (dismissively) by an alternative abbreviation can-p'ún (ကြံ့ဖွံ့.).

THE WALLS HAVE EARS

Because so many people in Myanmar are believed to be informers for Military Intelligence (MI) – some estimates put this at as many as one in ten of the adult population – Burmese people tend not to discuss sensitive subjects like politics in the presence of strangers or people other than close and trusted friends. When talking in public places, such as teashops, they will often be keeping an eye out for potential MI informers.

FEELINGS

ခံစားချက်များ

I'm ...	cănaw/cămá ...	ကျွန်တော်/ကျွန်မ
	ba-deh (m/f)	... ပါတယ်။
Are you ...?	... thălà/dhălà?	... သလား။
afraid	sò-yein	စိုးရိမ်
angry	seiq-s'ò	စိတ်ဆိုး
cold	c'àn	ချမ်း
depressed	seiq-daq cá	စိတ်ဓါတ်ကျ
furious	dàw-thá p'yiq	ဒေါသဖြစ်
happy	pyaw	ပျော်
hot	aiq	အိုက်
in a hurry	ălyin-sălo p'yiq	အလျင်စလို ဖြစ်
keen to ...	ăyàn seiq-win-sà	အရမ်း စိတ်ဝင်စား
right	hman	မှန်
sad	seiq-măkaùn	စိတ်မကောင်း
shy	sheq	ရှက်
sleepy	eiq-c'in	အိပ်ချင်
terrified	cauq	ကြောက်
thirsty	ye-ngaq	ရေငတ်
tired	pin-bàn	ပင်ပန်း
well	ne-kaùn	နေကောင်း
worried	seiq-pu	စိတ်ပူ

YOU & I

Women should use **shin** ('you') when addressing someone, and **cămá** ('I') for the first person.

Men should use **k'ămyà** for 'you' and **cănaw** for 'I'.

These words are appropriate for most situations but should not be used when speaking to monks (see page 47).

BREAKING THE LANGUAGE BARRIER

ဘာသာစကား အဟန့်အတား
ချိုးဖောက်ခြင်း

I'm looking for ...
   ... sha-ne-ba-deh
... ရှာနေပါတယ်။

Do you understand?
   nà-leh-dhălà?
နားလည်သလား။

I understand.
   nà-leh-ba-deh
နားလည်ပါတယ်။

I don't understand.
   nà-mǎleh-ba-bù
နားမလည်ပါဘူး။

Please say it again.
   pyan-pyàw-ba-oùn
ပြန်ပြောပါအုံး။

What do you call this in Burmese?
   da bǎma-lo beh-lo
   k'aw-dhǎlèh?
ဒါ ဗမာလို ဘယ်လိုခေါ်သလဲ။

Could you speak more slowly?
   p'yè-byè pyàw-ba naw?
ဖြေးဖြေးပြောပါနော်

Could you repeat that?
   t'aq-pyàw-ba-oùn?
ထပ်ပြောပါအုံး

Please write it down.
   yè-pyá-ba
ရေးပြပါ

What does ... mean?
   ... ba so-lo-da-lèh?
... ဘာ ဆိုလိုတာလဲ။

MEETING PEOPLE

I speak ...
  ... pyàw-daq-teh   ... ပြောတတ်တယ်။

I can't speak ...	... mǎpyàw-daq-pù	... မပြောတတ်ဘူး။
Can you speak ...?	(k'ǎmyà/shin) ...	ခင်ဗျား/ရှင် ...
	pyàw-daq-thǎlà? (m/f)	ပြောတတ်သလား။
Burmese	bǎma-zǎgà	ဗမာစကား
English	ìn-gǎleiq-zǎgà	အင်္ဂလိပ်စကား
French	pyin-thiq-zǎgà	ပြင်သစ်စကား
Japanese	jǎpan-zǎgà	ဂျာပန်စကား

Yes, I can.
  pyàw-daq-pa-deh   ပြောတတ်ပါတယ်။

No, I can't.
  mǎpyàw-daq-pa-bù   မပြောတတ်ပါဘူး။

I only speak a little.
  nèh-nèh pyàw-daq-ba-deh   နဲနဲ ပြောတတ်ပါတယ်။

MEETING PEOPLE

လှည့်ပတ်သွား လာခြင်း

GETTING AROUND

Plane, train, bus and car travel within Myanmar can be arranged by a travel company, your hotel or direct. Most 'taxis' are old jeeps, pick-ups or cars. Increasingly there are new saloon cars functioning as taxis, particularly in Yangon (Rangoon). As there are no meters, you should bargain for the price before you get in. Buses can be extremely crowded, although there are more and more new express air-con buses. For trips that can't be made by plane or train, shared jeeps or pick-ups are probably best.

FINDING YOUR WAY — လမ်းရှာဖွေခြင်း

Where is the ...?	... beh-hma-lèh?	... ဘယ်မှာလဲ။
airport	le-zeiq	လေဆိပ်
railway station	bu-da-youn	ဘူတာရုံ
bus station	baq-săkà-geiq	ဘတ်စကားဂိတ်
riverboat jetty	thìn-bàw-zeiq	သင်္ဘောဆိပ်

What ... is this?	da ba ... lèh?	ဒါ ဘာ ... လဲ။
town	myó	မြို့
street	làn	လမ်း
bus	baq-săkà	ဘတ်စကား

When will the ... leave?	... beh-ăc'ein t'weq-mălèh?	... ဘယ်အချိန် ထွက်မလဲ။
plane	le-yin-byan	လေယာဉ်ပျံ
train	mì-yăt'à	မီးရထား
bus	baq-săkà	ဘတ်စကား
riverboat	thìn-bàw	သင်္ဘော
jeep	jiq-kà	ဂျစ်ကား
taxi	ăhngà-kà/teq-si	အငှါးကား/ တက္ကစီ

How do I get to ...?
... ko beh-lo thwà-yá-dhălèh? ... ကို ဘယ်လိုသွားရသလဲ။

Can I get there by ...?	**... néh thwà-ló yá-mălà?**	... နဲ့ သွားလို့ရမလား။
taxi	**ăhngà-kà/teq-si**	အငှါးကား/တက္ကစီ
bus	**baq-săkà**	ဘတ်စကား
bicycle	**seq-beìn**	စက်ဘီး

Can I walk there?
làn-shauq-yin yá-mălà? လမ်းလျှောက်ရင် ရမလား။

Is this the way to ...?
di-làn ... thwà-téh-làn-là? ဒီလမ်း ... သွားတဲ့လမ်းလား။

Is it nearby?
di-nà-hma-là? ဒီနားမှာလား။

Is it far?
wè-dhălà? ဝေးသလား။

How far away is it?
beh-lauq wè-dhălèh? ဘယ်လောက်ဝေးသလဲ။

Can you show me (on the map)?
(mye-boun-hma) hnyun-pyá-pè-ba? (မြေပုံမှာ) ညွှန်ပြပေးပါ။

DIRECTIONS ဦးတည်ရာလမ်းကြောင်း

left	**beh-beq**	ဘယ်ဘက်
right	**nya-beq**	ညာဘက်
straight (ahead)	**téh-déh**	တည့်တည့်
very far away	**theiq wè-deh**	သိပ်ဝေးတယ်။
not so far away	**theiq măwè-bù**	သိပ်မဝေးဘူး။
north	**myauq-p'eq**	မြောက်ဘက်
south	**taun-beq**	တောင်ဘက်
east	**ăshé-beq**	အရှေ့ ဘက်
west	**ănauq-p'eq**	အနောက်ဘက်

TAXI

အငှါးကား/တက္ကစီ

In most towns, bicycle rickshaws, known as 'trishaws' or 'side-cars', are still popular. They can take one (regular-sized) or two (small) passengers. Fares should be negotiated upfront. In larger cities, such as Yangon and Mandalay, they are no longer able to travel in certain downtown areas. In rural areas, as well as the tourist sites of Bagan and Pyin-Oo-Lwin (Maymyo), pony carts are the preferred form of short-distance public transport.

Is this ... free?	... à-là?	... အား လား။
car	kà	ကား
pony cart	myìn-hlèh	မြင်းလှည်း
taxi	ăhngà-kà/teq-si	အငှါးကား/တက္ကစီ
trishaw	s'aiq-kà	ဆိုက်ကား

Please take me to ...
    ... ko thwà-jin-ba-deh   ... ကို သွားချင်ပါတယ်။
How much is the fare?
    kà-gá beh-lauq-lèh?   ကားခ ဘယ်လောက်လဲ။

Instructions

လမ်းညွှန်ချက်များ

Please load my bag.
    thiq-ta tin-pè-ba   သေတ္တာတင်ပေးပါ။
Continue!
    s'eq-thwà-ba-oùn!   ဆက်သွားပါအုံး။
The next street to the left/right.
    shé-làn-hma beh/nya kwé-ba   ရှေ့လမ်းမှာ ဘယ်/ညာ ကွေ့ပါ။
Please go slowly.
    pyè-byè thwà-ba   ပြည်းပြည်းသွားပါ။
Please wait for me.
    cănaw/cămá-go saún-ne-ba (m/f)   ကျွန်တော်/ကျွန်မကိုစောင့်နေပါ။
Stop here.
    di-hma yaq-pa   ဒီမှာ ရပ်ပါ။
Go to the corner of Fifth Street.
    ngà-làn-daún-go thwà-ba   ငါးလမ်းထောင့်ကို သွားပါ။

GETTING AROUND

BUYING TICKETS   လက်မှတ်ဝယ်ခြင်း

Where can I buy a ticket?
leq-hmaq beh-hma   လက်မှတ် ဘယ်မှာဝယ်ရမလဲ။
weh-yá-mǎlèh?

I'd like to book a seat to ...
... ko thwà-bó t'ain-goun   ... ကို သွားဖို့
co-yu-jin-ba-deh   ထိုင်ခုံကြိုယူချင်ပါတယ်။

It's full.
pyé-ne-bi   ပြည့်နေပြီ။

I would like ...	cănaw/cămá ...	ကျွန်တော်/ကျွန်မ ...
	lo-jin-ba-deh (m/f)	လိုချင်ပါတယ်။
a one-way ticket	ăthwà leq-hmaq	အသွားလက်မှတ်
a return ticket	ăthwà-ăpyan	အသွားအပြန်
	leq-hmaq	လက်မှတ်
one ticket	leq-hmaq tăzaun	လက်မှတ်တစ်စောင်
two tickets	leq-hmaq hnăzaun	လက်မှတ်နှစ်စောင်
a sleeper (a bed)	eiq-ya	အိပ်ရာ
a compartment/	ăk'àn	အခန်း
cabin (on a boat)		
upper class	ăt'eq-tàn	အထက်တန်း
ordinary class	yò-yò-dàn	ရိုးရိုးတန်း

AIR   လေကြောင်း

Is there a flight to ...?
... ko thwà-bó le-yin shí-là?   ... ကိုသွားဖို့ လေယာဉ်ရှိလား။

When's the next flight to ...?
... ko thwà-bó nauq-le-yin   ... ကိုသွားဖို့ နောက်လေယာဉ်
beh-ăc'ein-shí-lèh?   ဘယ်အချိန်ရှိလဲ။

How long does the flight take?
pyan-thàn-jein   ပျံသန်းချိန်
beh-lauq-ca-lèh?   ဘယ်လောက်ကြာလဲ။

What time do I have to check
in at the airport?
  le-zeiq-hma c'eq-in
  beh-ăc'ein-louq-yá-mălèh?
လေဆိပ်မှာ ချက်အင်
ဘယ်အချိန်လုပ်ရမလဲ။

My luggage hasn't arrived.
  cănáw/cămá eiq-twe
  măyauq-thè-bù (m/f)
ကျွန်တော်/ကျွန်မ အိတ်တွေ
မရောက်သေးဘူး။

At Customs
အကောက်အခွန်ရုံးမှာ

I have nothing to declare.
  ăk'un s'aun-săya măpa-bù
အခွန်ဆောင်စရာ မပါဘူး။

I have something to declare.
  ăk'un s'aun-săya tăk'ú-gú pa-deh
အခွန်ဆောင်စရာ တစ်ခုခုပါတယ်။

Do I have to declare this?
  di-ha-go ăk'un s'aun-yá-mălà?
ဒီဟာကို အခွန်ဆောင်ရမလား။

That's not mine.
  di-ha cănáw-ha măhouq-p'ù (m)
ဒီဟာ ကျွန်တော့်ဟာ မဟုတ်ဘူး။

I didn't know I had to declare it.
  di-ha-go ăk'un s'aun-săya
  măthí-ló-ba
ဒီဟာကို အခွန်ဆောင်စရာ
မသိလို့ပါ။

BUS
ဘတ်စ်ကား

Where does this bus go?
  di baq-săkà beh-go
  thwà-dhălèh?
ဒီဘတ်စ်ကား
ဘယ်ကိုသွားသလဲ။

Where should I get off?
  beh-hma s'ìn-yá-mălèh?
ဘယ်မှာဆင်းရမလဲ။

Which bus goes to ...?
  ... ko beh-baq-săkà
  thwà-mălèh?
... ကို ဘယ်ဘတ်စ်ကား
သွားမလဲ။

Bus No 8 goes there.
  baq-săkà nan-baq-shiq
  ho-beq thwà-deh
ဘတ်စ်ကား နံပါတ်ရှစ်
ဟိုဘက် သွားတယ်။

GETTING AROUND

How often do buses come?
  beh-hnănayi tăsì shí-lèh?   ဘယ်နှစ်နာရီတစ်စီး ရှိလဲ။

Could you let me know when
we get to ...?
  yauq-dé-ăc'ein
  pyàw-pè-nain-mălà?   ရောက်တဲ့အချိန်
  ပြောပေးနိုင်မလား။

BOAT   သင်္ဘော

Where does the boat leave from?
  thìn-bàw beh-ga t'weq-mălèh?   သင်္ဘော ဘယ်ကထွက်မလဲ။

What time does the boat arrive?
  thìn-bàw beh-ăc'ein
  yauq-mălèh?   သင်္ဘော
  ဘယ်အချိန်ရောက်မလဲ။

What time does the boat leave?
  thìn-bàw beh-ăc'ein
  t'weq-mălèh?   သင်္ဘော ဘယ်အချိန်ထွက်မလဲ။

TRAIN   မီးရထား

What station is this?
  da ba-bu-da-lèh?   ဒါဘာဘူတာလဲ။

What's the next station?
  nauq ba-bu-da-lèh?   နောက်ဘာဘူတာလဲ။

The train is delayed.
  yăt'à nauq-cá-deh   ရထားနောက်ကျတယ်။

The train is cancelled.
  kăyì-zin p'yaq-teh   ခရီးစဉ်ဖျက်တယ်။

How many hours is it by train
to Mandalay?
  màn-dălè-go yăt'à-néh
  beh-lauq ca-ja
  thwà-yá-dhà-lèh?   မန္တလေးကို ရထားနဲ့
  ဘယ်လောက်
  ကြာကြာသွားရလဲ။

Is that seat taken?
  di koun yu-t'à-bi-là?   ဒီခုံယူထားပြီလား။

CAR
ကား

It's not possible to hire a car without a driver and you probably wouldn't want to – driving in Myanmar takes a certain skill, as does finding petrol.

Where can I hire a car (and driver)?
kà(néh drai-ba) beh-hma ngà-ló yá-mălèh? ကား(နဲ့ ဒရိုင်ဘာ) ဘယ်မှာ ငှားလို့ ရမလဲ။

How much is it daily/weekly?
tăyeq/tăpaq beh-lauq-lèh? တစ်ရက်/တစ်ပတ် ဘယ်လောက်လဲ။

Is that price all-inclusive?
zè-deh-hma à-loùn pa-thălà? ဈေးထဲမှာအားလုံးပါသလား။

How much does it cost per mile?
tămain-ko beh-lauq-lèh? တစ်မိုင်ကိုဘယ်လောက်လဲ။

I'll pay half now, and half at the end of the trip.
ăk'ú tăweq pè-t'à-meh, can tăweq k'ăyì-s'oùn-yin pè-meh အခုတစ်ဝက် ပေးထားမယ်၊ ကျန်တစ်ဝက် ခရီးဆုံးရင် ပေးမယ်။

I'd like to see the car.
kà-go cí-jin-deh ကားကိုကြည့်ချင်တယ်။

I'd like to meet the driver.
drai-ba-néh twé-jin-deh ဒရိုင်ဘာနဲ့ တွေ့ချင်တယ်။

How many people does the vehicle take?
lu-beh-hnăyauq-sì-kà-lèh? လူဘယ်နှစ်ယောက်စီးကားလဲ။

Are there checkpoints on the road?
làn-hma sha-p'we-yè ăp'wéh shí-là? လမ်းမှာရှာဖွေရေးအဖွဲ့ရှိလား။

BICYCLE စက်ဘီး

Is it within cycling distance?
  seq-beìn-néh thwà-lauq-aun nì-là? စက်ဘီးနဲ့ သွားလောက်အောင် နီးလား။

Is there a bike lane?
  seq-beìn-làn shí-là? စက်ဘီးလမ်း ရှိလား။

Where can I hire a bicycle?
  seq-beìn beh-hma ngà-ló yá-mălèh? စက်ဘီးဘယ်မှာငှါးလို့ရမလဲ။

Where can I buy a (secondhand) bicycle?
  seq-beìn(-haùn) beh-hma weh-ló-yá-mălèh? စက်ဘီး(ဟောင်း) ဘယ်မှာဝယ်လို့ရမလဲ။

How much is it for ...?	... ko beh-lauq-lèh?	... ကိုဘယ်လောက်လဲ။
an hour	tănayi	တစ်နာရီ
the morning	tămăneq	တစ်မနက်
the afternoon	tăné-gìn	တစ်နေ့ခင်း
the day	tăné	တစ်နေ့

I have a flat tyre.
  beìn pauq-ne-deh ဘီးပေါက်နေတယ်။

Can I have a pump?
  le-t'ò-paiq yá-mălà? လေထိုးပိုက် ရမလား။

Can you pump up the tyres?
  le-t'ò-pè-nain-mălà? လေထိုးပေးနိုင်မလား။

The brakes don't work.
  breiq mămí-bù ဘရိတ်မမိဘူး။

THE FRONT SEAT

If you take a 4WD pick-up or 'line car' (laìn-kà, လိုင်းကား), it is usually more comfortable to travel in the shé-gàn (ရှေ့ခန်း), literally 'front room'. You may have to pay twice as much as to travel in the back, but it's worth it. These seats are often occupied by monks, however.

SOME USEFUL PHRASES   အသုံးဝင်သောဝေါဟာရများ

Can I sit here?
  di-hma t'ain-ló yá-là?   ဒီမှာထိုင်လို့ ရလား။

Can I put my things here?
  cănáw/cămá pyiq-sí-de
  di-hma t'à-ló yá-là? (m/f)   ကျွန်တော့်/ကျွန်မ ပစ္စည်းတွေ
  ဒီမှာ ထားလို့ ရလား။

How much is it to go
to Monywa?
  mon-ywa thwà-yin
  beh-lauq-lèh?   မုံရွာသွားရင် ဘယ်လောက်လဲ။

I'd like to sit in the front.
  shé-gàn-hma t'ain-jin-deh   ရှေ့ခန်းမှာထိုင်ချင်တယ်။

Can I get on board now?
(buses, boats etc)
  ăk'ú teq-ló yá-là?   အခု တက်လို့ရလား။

What time will we reach
Bagan (Pagan)?
  băgan beh-ăc'ein yauq-mălèh?   ပုဂံ ဘယ်အချိန် ရောက်မလဲ။

GETTING AROUND

SOME USEFUL WORDS   အသုံးဝင်သောစကားလုံးများ

address	leiq-sa	လိပ်စာ
bicycle	seq-beìn	စက်ဘီး
boat deck	koùn-baq	ကုန်းပတ်
buy	weh-deh	ဝယ်တယ်
cabin/compartment	ăk'àn	အခန်း
corner	daún	ထောင့်
early (adv)	sàw-zàw	စောစော
early (v/adj)	sàw-deh	စောတယ်
express train	ămyan yăt'à	အမြန်ရထား
far	wè-deh	ဝေးတယ်
fast	myan-deh	မြန်တယ်
hire	hngà-deh	ငှါးတယ်
house number	ein-nan-baq	အိမ်နံဘတ်
late	nauq-cá-deh	နောက်ကျတယ်
local train	law-keh yăt'à	လော်ကယ်ရထား
motorcycle	mo-ta s'ain-keh	မော်တော်ဆိုင်ကယ်
near	nì-deh	နီးတယ်
railway carriage	mì-yăt'à-dwèh	မီးရထားတွဲ
rickshaw/side-car	s'aiq-kà	ဆိုက်ကား
sit	t'ain-deh	ထိုင်တယ်
slow	hnè-deh	နှေးတယ်

နေရာထိုင်ခြင်း ACCOMMODATION

Nowadays, there's a range of small private guesthouses and travel agencies that arrange for someone to meet most flights and trains. Many new private hotels have sprung up in recent years and, as some of these are joint ventures, they can be booked directly from overseas.

FINDING ACCOMMODATION

နေရာထိုင်ခင်းရှာဖွေခြင်း

Is there a ... near here?	... di-nà-hma shí-là?	... ဒီနားမှာရှိလား။
hotel	ho-teh	ဟိုတယ်
guesthouse	tèh-k'o-gàn	တည်းခိုခန်း

Where can I find a/an ... hotel?	... ho-teh beh-nà-hma shí-lèh?	... ဟိုတယ် ဘယ်နားမှာ ရှိလဲ။
clean	thán-déh	သန့်တဲ့
good	kaùn-déh	ကောင်းတဲ့
inexpensive	zè theq-tha-déh	ဈေးသက်သာတဲ့

What's the address?
   beh leiq-sa-lèh?   ဘယ်လိပ်စာလဲ။

Could you write the address, please?
   leiq-sa yè-pyá-ba?   လိပ်စာရေးပြပါ။

BOOKING AHEAD

အခန်းကြိုယူခြင်း

I'd like to book a room, please.

ăk'àn tăkàn co-yu-jin-ba-deh   အခန်းတစ်ခန်းကြိုယူချင်ပါတယ်။

How much is the room for
one night?

ăk'àn tăyeq-ko   အခန်း တစ်ရက်ကို
beh-lauq-lèh?   ဘယ်လောက်လဲ။

How much is ...	... beh-lauq-lèh?	... ဘယ်လောက်လဲ။
one night	tăyeq	တစ်ရက်
two nights	hnăyeq	နှစ်ရက်
a single room	tăyauq-k'an	တစ်ယောက်ခန်း
a double room	hnăyauq-k'an	နှစ်ယောက်ခန်း
a cheaper room	zè-po-nèh-déh ăk'an	ဈေးပို့နဲ့တဲ့အခန်း
breakfast	măneq-sa	မနက်စာ
lunch	né-leh-za	နေ့လယ်စာ
dinner	nyá-za	ညစာ

Is breakfast included in the price?

ăk'an-g'á-dèh-hma   အခန်းခထဲမှာ မနက်စာ
măneq-sa pa-dhălà?   ပါသလား။

We'll be arriving at ...

cănaw-dó ...   ကျွန်တော်တို့ ...
ăc'ein-yauq-deh (m)   အချိန်ရောက်တယ်။

My name's ...

cănáw/cămá na-meh ... (m/f)   ကျွန်တော့်/ကျွမ နာမည် ...

I will stay for two nights.

hnăyeq tèh-meh   နှစ်ရက်တည်းမယ်။

CHECKING IN

ချက်အင်

Can foreigners stay here?

   nain-ngan-jà-thà di-hma   နိုင်ငံခြားသား
   tèh-ló yá-là?   ဒီမှာတည်းလို့ရလား။

Do you have any rooms available?

   thín-daw-téh ăk'àn shí-là?   သင့်တော်တဲ့အခန်းရှိလား။

Do you have a room with two beds?

   gădin-hnăloùn-pa-téh   ခုတင်နှစ်လုံးပါတဲ့ အခန်း
   ăk'an shí-là?   ရှိလား။

Do you have a room with a
double bed?

   hnăyauq-eiq-gădin-pa-téh   နှစ်ယောက်အိပ်ခုတင်ပါတဲ့
   ăk'an shí-là?   အခန်း ရှိလား။

Sorry, we're full.

   seiq-măshí-ba-néh   စိတ်မရှိပါနဲ့၊ကျွန်တော်တို့
   cănaw-dó ăk'àn-dwe   အခန်းတွေပြည့်နေပါတယ်။
   pyé-ne-ba-deh

(I/We) want a	... néh ăk'àn-tăkàn	... နဲ့ အခန်းတစ်ခန်း
room with (a) ...	lo-jin-ba-deh	လိုချင်ပါတယ်။
air-conditioning	èh-kùn	အဲကွန်း
bathroom	ye-c'ò-gàn	ရေချိုးခန်း
hot water	ye-nwè	ရေနွေး
mosquito net	c'in-daun	ခြင်ထောင်
telephone	p'oùn	ဖုန်း
toilet	ein-dha	အိမ်သာ
TV	ti-vi	တီဗွီ

ACCOMMODATION

TOWELLING DOWN

Since the lower part of the body is regarded as less clean than the head, you should use separate towels for your face and body, and not wash your feet in basins used for the rest of your body.

ACCOMMODATION

Do you have a better room?
po-kaùn-déh-ăk'àn shí-là?
ပိုကောင်းတဲ့အခန်း ရှိလား။

May I see the room?
ăk'àn cí-ba-yá-se?
အခန်း ကြည့်ပါရစေ။

It's fine. I'll take it.
ăs'in-pye-ba-deh, cănaw
yu-meh (m)
အဆင်ပြေပါတယ်၊
ကျွန်တော်ယူမယ်။

Is there hot water all day?
ye-nwè-ye-jò-gàn tăne-goun
thoùn-ló-yá-là?
ရေနွေးရေချိုးခန်း
တစ်နေ့ကုန်သုံးလို့ရလား။

Can I pay in kyats?
caq-néh pè-ló yá-là?
ကျပ်နဲ့ပေးလို့ရလား။

This room is good.
di ăk'àn kaùn-deh
ဒီအခန်း ကောင်းတယ်။

I/We'll stay here.
di-hma tèh-meh
ဒီမှာ တည်းမယ်။

We'll stay together.
ătu-du tèh-meh
အတူတူ တည်းမယ်။

We'll stay in separate rooms.
tăyauq-tăk'àn-si
tèh-meh
တစ်ယောက်တစ်ခန်းစီ
တည်းမယ်။

REQUESTS & COMPLAINTS

တောင်းခံမှုနှင့်တင်ပြမှုများ

Can I leave a message?
message t'à-kéh-ló yá-là?
မက်ဆ့်ချ် ထားခဲ့လို့ ရလား။

Is there a message for me?
cănaw ătweq
message shí-là? (m)
ကျွန်တော်အတွက်
မက်ဆ့်ချ် ရှိလား။

Where can I get my clothes washed?
ăwuq beh-hma shaw-ló
yá-dhălèh?
အဝတ် ဘယ်မှာလျှော်လို့ရသလဲ။

Could we have …? ... yá-nain-mălà? ... ရနိုင်မလား။
 an extra blanket s'aun ăpo ဆောင်အပို
 our key cănaw-dó tháw ကျွန်တော်တို့သော့

Do you serve breakfast?
 măneq-sa cwè-dhălà? မနက်စာကျွေးသလား။
The room is expensive.
 ăk'àn zè-jì-deh အခန်း ဈေးကြီးတယ်။
There are four of us.
 cănaw-dó/cămá-dó ကျွန်တော်တို့/ ကျွန်မတို့
 lè-yauq shí-deh (m/f) လေးယောက်ရှိတယ်။
Where is the bathroom?
 ye-c'ò-gàn beh-hma-lèh? ရေချိုးခန်း ဘယ်မှာလဲ။
Please fix the light.
 mì pyin-pè-ba မီးပြင်ပေးပါ။

I've locked myself out of my room.
 ăkàn-dèh-hma cănáw tháw အခန်းထဲမှာ
 mé-géh-deh (m) ကျွန်တော်သော့မေ့ခဲ့တယ်။
We left the key at reception.
 cănaw-dó reception-hma tháw ကျွန်တော်တို့ ရပ်စရှင်းမှာ
 t'à-géh-ba-deh (m) သော့ထားခဲ့ပါတယ်။
I can't open/close the window.
 pădìn-bauq p'wín/ ပြတင်းပေါက် ဖွင့်/ပိတ်လို့
 paiq-ló măyá-bù မရဘူး။
I don't like this room.
 di ăkàn-go măcaiq-p'u ဒီအခန်းကို မကြိုက်ဘူး။
The toilet won't flush.
 ein-dha ye-swèh-ló măyá-bù အိမ်သာ ရေဆွဲလို့ မရဘူး။

It's too ...	ăyàn ... ba-deh	အရမ်း ... ပါတယ်။
cold	è	အေး
dark	hmaun	မှောင်
expensive	zè-cì	ဈေးကြီး
light/bright	lìn	လင်း
noisy	s'u-nyan	ဆူညံ
small	cìn	ကျဉ်း

The room needs to be cleaned.
ăkàn-thán-shìn-yè louq-p'ó
lo-deh

အခန်းသန့်ရှင်းရေး
လုပ်ဖို့လိုတယ်။

Is there a ...	... di-nà-hma	... ဒီနားမှာရှိလား။
near here?	shí-là?	
food stall	sà-thauq-s'ain	စားသောက်ဆိုင်
restaurant	sà-daw-s'eq	စားတော်ဆက်

CHECKING OUT   ချက်အောက်/ထွက်ခွာခြင်း

What time do we have to check out?
beh ăc'ein checkout
louq-yá-mălèh?

ဘယ်အချိန် ချက်အောက်
လုပ်ရမလဲ။

(I'm/We're) leaving now.
ăkú pyan-táw-meh

အခုပြန်တော့မယ်။

We had a great stay, thank you.
di-hma ne-yá-da
ăyàn-kaùn-ba-deh

ဒီမှာနေရတာ
အရမ်းကောင်းပါတယ်။

Thank you for all your help.
k'in-byà-yéh ku-nyi-hmú
à-loùn-ătweq c'è-zù-ba-bèh

ခင်ဗျားရဲ့ကူညီမှု အားလုံးအတွက်
ကျေးဇူးပါပဲ။

The room was perfect.
ăk'àn pyé-zoun-ba-deh

အခန်း ပြည့်စုံပါတယ်။

We hope we can return some day.
tăné pyan-la-p'yiq-meh
t'in-deh

တစ်နေ့ပြန်လာဖြစ်မယ်
ထင်တယ်။

I'd like to pay the bill.
   ngwe shìn-jin-ba-deh   ငွေရှင်းချင်ပါတယ်။

Can I pay by credit card?
   credit-kaq-néh pè-nain-mǎlà?   ခရက်ဒစ်ကတ်နဲ့ ပေးနိုင်မလား။

There's a mistake in the bill.
   pye-za-hma ǎhmà pa-ne-deh   ပြေစာမှာ အမှားပါနေတယ်။

Can I/we leave my/our bag(s)
for three days?
   thiq-ta di-hma thoùn-yeq   သေတ္တာ ဒီမှာ
   t'à-ló yá-dhǎlà?   သုံးရက်ထားလို့ရသလား။

I will come back in one week.
   tǎpaq-ǎdwìn   တစ်ပတ်အတွင်း
   pyan-la-oùn-meh   ပြန်လာအုံးမယ်။

Can you call a taxi for me?
   taxi k'aw-pè-nain-mǎlà?   တက္ကစီ ခေါ်ပေးနိုင်မလား။

ACCOMMODATION

SOME USEFUL WORDS   အသုံးဝင်သောစကားလုံးများ

blanket	saun	စောင်
candle	p'ǎyaùn-dain	ဖယောင်းတိုင်
clean	thán-deh	သန့်တယ်
dirty	nyiq-paq-deh	ညစ်ပတ်တယ်
door	dǎgà	တံခါး
fan (electric)	pan-ka	ပန်ကာ
fan (manual)	yaq-taun	ယပ်တောင်
key	tháw	သော့
noisy	s'u-nyan-deh	ဆူညံတယ်
padlock	tháw-gǎlauq	သော့လောက်
pillow	gaùn-oùn	ခေါင်းအုံး
plug (for sink)	ǎs'ó	အဆို့
quiet (peaceful)	s'eiq-nyein-deh	ဆိတ်ငြိမ်တယ်
roof	ǎmò	အမိုး
sheet	eiq-ya-k'ìn	အိပ်ရာခင်း

shower	ye-bàn	ရေပန်း
sleep	eiq-teh	အိပ်တယ်
soap	s'aq-pya	ဆပ်ပြာ
suitcase/box	thiq-t'a	သေတ္တာ
tap	ye-boun-bain	ရေဘုံပိုင်
towel	myeq-hna-thouq-păwa	မျက်နာသုတ်ပဝါ
wash (body)	ye-c'ò-deh	ရေချိုးတယ်
wash (clothes)	ăwuq-shaw-deh	အဝတ်လျှော်တယ်
wash (face)	myeq-hna thiq-teh	မျက်နာ သစ်တယ်
wash (hair)	gaùn-shaw-deh	ခေါင်းလျှော်တယ်

ACCOMMODATION

SHOES OFF

When you enter a house, a monastery or a temple precinct,
you should take your shoes and socks off. In some temples
you can carry them with you. In others, it may be more
appropriate to leave them at the door.

AROUND TOWN

It's not hard to find your way round the towns in Myanmar. Tourist maps are available in Yangon, Mandalay and Bagan and you'll find many street signs are in English. In downtown Yangon you can orient yourself by the central landmark – the Sule Pagoda. The word for street is làn.

LOOKING FOR ...   ... ရှာဖွေခြင်း

Where is the ...?	... beh-hma-lèh?	... ဘယ်မှာလဲ။
bank	ban-daiq	ဘဏ်တိုက်
market	zè	ဈေး
museum	pyá-daiq	ပြတိုက်
post office	sa-daiq	စာတိုက်

How far is the ...?	... beh-lauq wè-dhălèh?	... ဘယ်လောက် ဝေးသလဲ။
bookshop	sa-ouq-s'ain	စာအုပ်ဆိုင်
botanical garden	youq-k'á-be-dá ú-yin	ရုက္ခဗေဒဥယျာဉ်
church	p'ăyà-shí-k'ò-caùn	ဘုရားရှိခိုးကျောင်း
cinema	youq-shin-youn	ရုပ်ရှင်ရုံ
monastery	p'oùn-jì-caùn	ဘုန်းကြီးကျောင်း
park	pàn-jan	ပန်းခြံ
university	teq-kătho	တက္ကသိုလ်

I would like to buy a map.

| mye-boun-dăboun weh-jin-ba-deh | မြေပုံတစ်ပုံဝယ်ချင်ပါတယ်။ |

AT THE BANK   ဘဏ်တိုက်မှာ

Official exchange rates are fixed and some things (including most hotel accommodation and travel) must be paid for in hard currency or foreign exchange certificates (FECs). On arrival, you will be required to change some foreign currency into FECs (in Burmese 'FEC' or bă-ma daw-la).

What time does the bank open?
ban-daiq beh ăc'ein	ဘဏ်တိုက် ဘယ်အချိန်
pwín-mălèh?	ပွင့်မလဲ။

I want to ... lèh-jin-ba-deh   ... လဲချင်ပါတယ်။
change ...

banknotes	ngwe seq-ku	ငွေစက္ကူ
dollars	daw-la	ဒေါ်လာ
foreign currency	nain-ngan-gyà ngwe	နိုင်ငံခြားငွေ
money	paiq-s'an	ပိုက်ဆံ
pounds	paun	ပေါင်
travellers cheques	k'ăyì-c'eq-leq-hmaq	ခရီးချက်လက်မှတ်

Can I use my credit card to withdraw money?
ngwe-t'ouq-p'ó cănaw	ငွေထုတ်ဖို့ ကျွန်တော်
credit-kaq-ko	ခရက်ဒစ်ကတ်ကို
thoùn-nain-mălà?	သုံးနိုင်မလား။

Can I cash a cheque?
c'eq-ko ngwe-lèh-pè-ló yá-là?	ချက်ကိုငွေလဲပေးလို့ရလား။

Please write it here.
di-hma yè-ba	ဒီမှာ ရေးပါ။

Please give me smaller bills/change.
ănouq lèh-pè-ba	အနုပ်လဲပေးပါ။

Where can I change money?
   paiq-s'an beh-hma lèh-ló   ပိုက်ဆံ ဘယ်မှာလဲလို့ရမလဲ။
   yá-mălèh?

How much will you give me for
a hundred dollars?
   daw-la tăya-go beh-lauq   ဒေါ်လာတစ်ရာကို ဘယ်လောက်
   pyan-pè-mălèh?   ပြန်ပေးမလဲ။

How many kyat to a dollar?
   dawla-zè beh-lauq-lèh?   ဒေါ်လာဈေး ဘယ်လောက်လဲ။

Where do I sign?
   beh-ne-ya-hma leq-hmaq   ဘယ်နေရာမှာ လက်မှတ်
   t'ò-yá-mălèh?   ထိုးရမလဲ။

AT THE POST OFFICE   စာတိုက်မှာ

I would like	... pó-jin-ba-deh	... ပို့ချင်ပါတယ်။
to send ...		
a/one letter	sa-tăzaun	စာတစ်စောင်
a/one parcel	pa-seh-tăt'ouq	ပါဆယ်တစ်ထုပ်
two postcards	pó-săkaq hnăzaun	ပို့စကတ်နှစ်စောင်

How much to	... pó-yin	... ပို့ရင်
send ...?	beh-lauq-lèh?	ဘယ်လောက်လဲ။
an airmail letter	le-jaùn-sa	လေကြောင်းစာ
express	ămyan	အမြန်
a fax	fax	ဖက်စ်
printed matter	sa-ouq-te	စာအုပ်တွေ
a registered letter	hmaq-poun-tin-za	မှတ်ပုံတင်စာ
surface	yò-yò	ရိုးရိုး

Please give me two 5-kyat stamps.
   ngà-caq-tan dăzeiq-gaùn   ငါးကျပ်တန်တံဆိပ်ခေါင်း
   hnăloùn pè-ba   နှစ်လုံးပေးပါ။

AROUND TOWN

Please give me two aerograms.
  èh-ya leq-ta   အဲယားလက်တာ
  hnǎyweq pè-ba   နှစ်ရွက် ပေးပါ။

I want to send this letter to
America.
  di-sa ǎme-rí-kà-go   ဒီစာ အမေရိကားကို
  pó-jin-deh   ပို့ချင်တယ်။

Can I send this by registered mail?
  hmaq-poun-tin pó-ló yá-là?   မှတ်ပုံတင်ပို့လို့ ရလား။

I want to send this letter by
airmail to France.
  di-sa le-jaùn-néh   ဒီစာ လေကြောင်းနဲ့
  pyin-thiq-pye-ko pó-jin-deh   ပြင်သစ်ပြည်ကို ပို့ချင်တယ်။

How much does it cost altogether?
  à-loùn beh-lauq-cá-lèh?   အားလုံး ဘယ်လောက်ကျလဲ။

Please give me   ... pè-ba   ... ပေးပါ။
a/an ...
  air-letter   èh-yà-leq-ta   အဲယားလက်တာ
  envelope   sa-eiq   စာအိတ်
  receipt   pye-za   ပြေစာ
  stamp   dǎzeiq-gaùn   တံဆိပ်ခေါင်းတစ်လုံး
                 tǎloùn
  telephone   teh-li-p'oùn   တယ်လီဖုန်းလမ်းညွှန်
    directory   làn-hnyun

AROUND TOWN

KYAT CHAT

The currency, kyat, is written in this book as caq. Pronounce
it as you would 'chat', but without sounding the 't' – just
stop the 'a' short with a catch in your voice. It's this sound
which has caused it to be romanised with a 't' on the end.

TELECOMMUNICATIONS ဆက်သွယ်ရေး

Can I send a fax?
  fax pó-ló yá-là? ဖက်စ်ပို့လို့ ရလား။

I would like to send a telegram/cable.
  cè-nàn tăk'ú pó-jin-ba-deh ကြေးနန်းတစ်ခု ပို့ချင်ပါတယ်။

If I send a telgram/cable, how much per word?
  cè-nàn-yaiq-yin sa-tăloùn beh-lauq-lèh? ကြေးနန်းရိုက်ရင် စာတစ်လုံး ဘယ်လောက်လဲ။

I'd like to make a call.
  p'oùn-s'eq-c'in-deh ဖုံးဆက်ချင်တယ်။

Please call this number for me.
  di teh-li-p'oùn nan-baq k'aw-pè-ba ဒီတယ်လီဖုံးနံပါတ်ခေါ်ပေးပါ။

How much does a (three)-minute call cost?
  ... (thoùn) măniq beh-lauq-lèh? ... (သုံး)မိနစ် ဘယ်လောက်လဲ။

The number is ...
  nan-baq-ká ... နံပါတ်က ...

What's the area code for ...?
  ... ătweq myó-nan-baq beh-lauq-lèh? ... အတွက် မြို့နံပါတ်ဘယ်လောက်လဲ။

I want to call ...	**... p'oùn k'aw-jin-ba-deh**	... ဖုန်းခေါ်ချင်ပါတယ်။
abroad	**nain-ngan-jà-go**	နိုင်ငံခြားကို
locally	**myó-dwìn**	မြို့တွင်း
long-distance	**neh-go**	နယ်ကို

It's engaged.
  laìn mă-à-bù လိုင်းမအားဘူး။

I've been cut off.
  laìn p'yaq-thwà-bi လိုင်းဖြတ်သွားပြီ။

SIGHTSEEING လှည့်လည်ကြည့်ရှုခြင်း

Burmese place and other names have conventional English versions, which may appear on signs and in guidebooks. In some cases, these can be different from the actual pronunciation of the places, and from their official anglicised names.

Where's the tourist office?
kăbá-hléh kăyì-thi-yoùn
beh-nà-mălèh?
ကမ္ဘာလှည့်ခရီးသည်ရုံး
ဘယ်နားမလဲ။

Is there an English-speaking guide?
ìngăleiq sägà-pyàw-daq-téh
gaiq shí-là?
အင်္ဂလိပ်စကားပြောတတ်တဲ့
ဂိုက် ရှိလား။

Can I take photographs?
daq-poun yaiq-ló yá-là?
ဓာတ်ပုံ ရိုက်လို့ရလား။

Could you take a photograph
of me?
cănaw-go daq-poun
yaiq-pè-nain-mălà? (m)
ကျွန်တော်ကို
ဓာတ်ပုံရိုက်ပေးနိုင်မလား။

Getting In ဝင်ခွင့်

How much is the entrance fee?
win-jè beh-lauq-lèh?
ဝင်ကြေး ဘယ်လောက်လဲ။

When will it open?
beh-dáw p'wín-mălèh?
ဘယ်တော့ဖွင့်မလဲ။

What time will it close?
beh-dáw peiq-mălèh?
ဘယ်တော့ပိက်မလဲ။

The Sights ရှုခင်းများ

What's that?
da-ba-lèh?
ဒါဘာလဲ။

When was it built?
beh-doùn-gá s'auq-thălèh?
ဘယ်တုန်းကဆောက်သလဲ။

Who built it?
bădhu s'auq-thălèh?
ဘယ်သူ ဆောက်သလဲ။

It's lovely!
   hlá-laiq-ta!   လှလိုက်တာ။

It's beautiful!
(said of pagodas, Buddhas etc)
   ci-nyo-zăya kaùn-deh!   ကြည့်သိုစရာ ကောင်းတယ်။

It's wonderful/very good!
   theiq kaùn-da-bèh!   သိပ် ကောင်းတာပဲ။

It's amazing!
   án-àw-zăya-bèh!   အံ့သြစရာပဲ။

It's strange!
   t'ù-zàn-laiq-ta!   ထူးဆန်းလိုက်တာ။

Main Sights in Yangon (Rangoon)
ရန်ကုန်မှာ အဓိကကြည့်စရာများ

Martyrs' Tomb	a-za-ni-goùn	အာဇာနည်ကုန်း
Shwedagon Pagoda	shwe-dăgoun p'ăyà	ရွှေတိဂုံဘုရား
Sule Pagoda	su-lè p'ăyà	ဆူးလေဘုရား
Inya Lake	ìn-yà-kan	အင်းလျားကန်
Royal Lake	kan-daw-jì	ကန်တော်ကြီး
Scott Market	bo-jouq-zè	ဗိုလ်ချုပ်ဈေး

AROUND TOWN

Main Sights in Mandalay
မန္တလေးမှာ အဓိကကြည့်စရာများ

Mandalay Palace	nàn-daw	နန်းတော်
Mahamuni Pagoda	măha-mú-ní-p'ăyà	မဟာမုနိဘုရား
Amarapura	á-má-rá-pu-rá	အမရပူရ
Mingun Bell	mìn-gùn-k'aùn-laùn	မင်းကွန်းခေါင်းလောင်း
Ava Bridge	ìn-wá-tădà	အင်းဝတံတား
Watchtower	hmyaw-zin	မျှော်စင်
Mandalay Hill	màn-dălè-taun	မန္တလေးတောင်
Central Market	zè-jo	ဈေးချို

Tours

လှည့်လည်ခြင်း

Can you arrange a tour to ... for me?
... ko leh-bó
si-zin-pè-nain-mălà?

... ကိုလည်ဖို့
စီစဉ်ပေးနိုင်မလား။

Can we hire a guide?
gaiq ngà-ló yá-là?

ဂိုက် ငှားလို့ရလား။

How much is the tour/a guide?
k'ăyì-zin/gaiq beh-lauq-lèh?

ခရီးစဉ်/ဂိုက် ဘယ်လောက်လဲ။

How long is the tour?
k'ăyì-zin beh-lauq-c'a-mălèh?

ခရီးစဉ် ဘယ်လောက်ကြာမလဲ။

How long are we here for?
di-hma beh-lauq-c'a-ja
ne-yá-mălèh?

ဒီမှာ
ဘယ်လောက်ကြာကြာနေရမလဲ။

What time should we be back?
beh ăc'ein cănaw-dó
pyan-yauq-mălèh? (m)

ဘယ်အချိန် ကျွန်တော်တို့
ပြန်ရောက်မလဲ။

The guide has paid/will pay.
gaiq pè-leín-meh

ဂိုက်ပေးလိမ့်မယ်။

I'm with them.
cănaw/cămá thu-dó-néh
ătu-la-deh (m/f)

ကျွန်တော်/ကျွမ သူတို့နဲ့
အတူလာတယ်။

SIGNS

ပိတ်ထားသည်	CLOSED
အဝင်	ENTRANCE
အထွက်	EXIT
မ	LADIES
ကျား	MEN
ဝင်ခွင့်မရှိ	NO ENTRY
ဆေးလိပ်မသောက်ရ	NO SMOKING
ဖွင့်သည်	OPEN
တားမြစ်နယ်မြေ	PROHIBITED (AREA)
အိမ်သာ/ရေအိမ်	TOILETS

GOING OUT အပြင်ထွက်ခြင်း

Burmese people generally get up before dawn, so they go to bed early – not least because many still don't have electric lights. Dinner is eaten by 6 or 7 pm. In most towns and villages in the countryside, the teashops and restaurants are closed by about 8 pm, and it's only when there are festivals and 'pwes' that people stay up later. In Yangon (Rangoon), there are now some late-night and even all-night teashops and discos, particularly in the big hotels.

In the evenings, families tend to watch TV or videos. Where electricity is limited, villages have a 'video hut' which has replaced the old travelling cinemas. In the towns, evening tuition classes to pass the high school exam or learn a foreign language or computing are also popular for those who can afford them.

What's there to do in the evenings?
nyá-gá ba louq-săya shí-lèh? ညက ဘာလုပ်စရာရှိလဲ။

I feel like going to a/the …	… go thwà-jin-seiq shí-deh	… ကို သွားချင်စိတ်ရှိတယ်။
bar	bà	ဘား
cinema	youq-shin-youn	ရုပ်ရှင်ရုံ
disco/night club	disco/naiq-kălaq	ဒစ္စကို/နိုက်ကလပ်
karaoke bar	ka-ra-o-ke-zain	ကာရာအိုကေဆိုင်
pwe	pwèh	ပွဲ
restaurant	sà-thauq-s'ain	စားသောက်ဆိုင်
teashop	lăp'eq-ye-zain	လက်ဖက်ရည်ဆိုင်
theatre	pyá-zaq	ပြဇာတ်
I feel like going …	… jin-seiq shí-deh	… ချင်စိတ် ရှိတယ်။
for a stroll	ăpyìn-pye-làn-shauq	အပျင်းပြေလမ်းလျှောက်
dancing	ká	က
for a coffee	kaw-fi thwà-thauq	ကော်ဖီသွားသောက်
for a beer	bi-ya thwà-thauq	ဘီယာသွားသောက်

Karaoke   ကာရာအိုကေ

Karaoke bars are becoming increasingly popular after-dinner activities throughout Myanmar, often set up informally in the back of someone's house or a restaurant. There is usually a mixture of Burmese and English-language songs on offer.

Do you have karaoke?
  ka-ra-o-ke shí-dhǎlà?   ကာရာအိုကေရှိသလား။

Which song do you want to sing?
  beh-thǎjìn-so-yá-da caiq-lèh?   ဘယ်သီချင်းဆိုရတာကြိုက်လဲ။

Do you like this song?
  di-thǎjìn caiq-là?   ဒီသီချင်းကြိုက်လား။

Do you want to sing this with me?
  cǎnaw/cǎma-néh kin-byà/   ကျွန်တော်/ကျွမနဲ့၊ ခင်ဗျား/
  shin soun-twèh so-mǎlà? (m/f)   ရှင် စုံတွဲဆိုမလား။

Who is this singer?
  di-ǎs'o-daw beh-thu-lèh?   ဒီအဆိုတော်ဘယ်သူလဲ။

You have a very good voice.
  ǎthan kaùn-deh   အသံကောင်းတယ်။

I can't sing very well.
  cǎnáw/cǎma ǎthan   ကျွန်တော်/ကျွမ အသံ
  theiq-mǎkaùn-bù (m/f)   သိပ်မကောင်းဘူး။

I'm a bit flat.
  ǎthan nèh-nèh   အသံနဲ့နဲ့ နိမ့်ကျသွားတယ်။
  neín-já-thwà-deh

SHOPPING

With the legalisation of border trade with Thailand, China and India, a wide range of Western toiletries and medicines has become available in the shops, often at prices lower than in the West. However, supplies and quality are erratic. If you have specific requirements, you should bring them with you.

Antiques must not be taken out of Myanmar, but most of what you will be offered only looks old anyway. Various handicrafts are available and the country is also a major exporter of teak, gems and jade.

LOOKING FOR ...   ... ရှာဖွေခြင်း

Where is the ...?	... beh-hma-lèh?	... ဘယ်မှာလဲ။
bookshop	sa-ouq-s'ain	စာအုပ်ဆိုင်
factory	seq-youn	စက်ရုံ
market	zè	ဈေး
pharmacy/chemist	s'è-zain	ဆေးဆိုင်
shop	s'ain	ဆိုင်

Where can I buy ...?	... beh-hma weh-yá-mălèh?	... ဘယ်မှာဝယ်ရမလဲ။
clothes	ăwuq-ăsà	အဝတ်အစား
books	sa-ouq-te	စာအုပ်တွေ
furniture	pări-bàw-gá	ပရိဘောဂ
gems	cauq-myeq/yădāna	ကျောက်မျက်/ရတနာ
lacquerware	yùn-deh	ယွန်းထည်
medicine	s'è	ဆေး

Do you have any ...?	... shí-là?	... ရှိလား။
matches	mì-jiq	မီးခြစ်
newspapers	thădìn-za-de	သတင်းစာတွေ
soap	s'aq-pya	ဆပ်ပြာ
thread	aq-c'i	အပ်ချည်

MAKING A PURCHASE   ဝယ်ယူခြင်း

I'm just looking.
cí-youn-ba-bèh   ကြည့်ရှုပါပဲ။

How much is ...?	... beh-lauq-lèh?	... ဘယ်လောက်လဲ။
one shirt	eìn-ji tǎt'eh	အကျီတစ်ထည်
two sewing needles	aq-hnǎc'aùn	အပ်နှစ်ချောင်း
four tickets	leq-hmaq lè-zaun	လက်မှတ်လေးစောင်
a pair of shoes	p'ǎnaq tǎyan	ဖိနပ်တစ်ရန်

If you want to use a number, you must put a counter word after it. Although there are quite a lot of counters used in Burmese, you can get by with a few. In general, k'ú (ခု) can be used for counting anything but people. See the Numbers chapter, page 153, for more details on how to use counters.

| two snacks | moún hnǎk'ú | မုန့်နှစ်ခု |
| three tickets | leq-hmaq thoùn-zaun | လက်မှတ်သုံးစောင် |

Can you write down the price?
zè-hnoùn-já-yè-pyá-ba?   ဈေးနှုန်းချရေးပြပေးပါ။

I'd like to buy ...
... weh-jin-ba-deh   ... ဝယ်ချင်ပါတယ်။

Do you have any others?
tǎjà-ha shí-thè-là?   တခြားဟာ ရှိသေးလား။

I don't really like it.
theiq-táw mǎcaiq-ba-bù   သိပ်တော့ မကြိုက်ပါဘူး။

SHOWING UNDERSTANDING

'I understand' is nà-leh-ba-deh;
'I don't understand' is nà-mǎ-leh-ba-bù.

BARGAINING

ဈေးဆစ်ခြင်း

Shopping means bargaining, except in government shops.

Please reduce the price.
zè-sháw-ba

ဈေးလျော့ပါ။

Please give me a bigger one.
po-cì-déh tǎk'ú pè-ba

ပိုကြီးတဲ့တခုပေးပါ။

Please give me a little one.
ǎthè tǎk'u pè-ba

အသေးတစ်ခု ပေးပါ။

It is very expensive.
zè theiq cì-deh

ဈေးသိပ်ကြီးတယ်။

Do you have a cheaper one?
zè po-pàw-dé tǎk'ú
shí-là?

ဈေးပိုပေါတဲ့တစ်ခု ရှိလား။

If I buy two, will you reduce
the price?
hnǎk'ú weh-yin,
zè-sháw-pè-mǎlà?

နှစ်ခုဝယ်ရင်
ဈေးလျော့ပေးမလား။

I will give you 100 (kyat).
tǎya pè-meh

တစ်ရာပေးမယ်။

That is not enough.
da mǎlauq-p'ù

ဒါ မလောက်ဘူး။

I have only 200 (kyat).
ngwe hnǎya-bèh shí-deh

ငွေနှစ်ရာဘဲ ရှိတယ်။

(You) must give me 300.
thoùn-ya pè-yá-meh

သုံးရာ ပေးရမယ်။

OK.
kaùn-ba-bi (lit: it is now good)

ကောင်းပါပြီ။

| expensive | zè-cì-deh | ဈေးကြီးတယ် |
| cheap | zè-pàw-deh | ဈေးပေါတယ် |

ESSENTIAL ITEMS

မရှိမဖြစ်ပစ္စည်းများ

I'd like (a) ...	... weh-jin-ba-deh	... ဝယ်ချင်ပါတယ်
batteries	daq-k'èh	ဓါတ်ခဲ
bread	paun-moún	ပေါင်မုန့်
butter	tàw-baq	ထောလတ်
camera	kin-măra	ကင်မရာ
candles	p'ăyaùn-dain	ဖယောင်းတိုင်
cheese	cheese	ချိစ်
chocolate	chàw-kălaq	ချောကလတ်
eggs	ú	ဥ
fan (manual)	yaq-taun	ယပ်တောင်
flour	joun	ဂျု
ham	weq-paun	ဝက်ပေါင်
honey	pyà-ye	ပျားရည်
lightbulb	mì-loùn	မီးလုံး
matches	mì-jiq	မီးခြစ်
milk	nwà-nó	နွားနို့
mosquito coil	c'in-zè-gwe	ခြင်ဆေးခွေ
pepper	ngăyouq-kaùn	ငရုတ်ကောင်း
radio	re-di-yo	ရေဒီယို
salt	s'à	ဆား
sugar	thăjà	သကြား
washing powder	s'aq-pya-hmoún	ဆပ်ပြာမှုန့်
yogurt	dein-jin	ဒိန်ချဉ်

LONGYI ETIQUETTE

As a 'nether garment', you should avoid placing your 'longyi' (sarong) close to your head. It should not, for example, be draped around your shoulders, and should be put on via the feet, not over the head.

SHOPPING

SOUVENIRS

အမှတ်တရပစ္စည်းများ

bag	eiq	အိတ်
basket	c'ìn-daùn	ခြင်းတောင်း
betel box	kùn-iq	ကွမ်းအစ်
bottle	pălìn	ပုလင်း
Burmese harp	saùn	စောင်း
chess	siq-băyin	စစ်တုရင်
cymbal	lăgwìn	လင်းကွင်း
earring	năgaq	နားကပ်
flute	pălwe	ပလွေ
lacquerware	yùn-deh	ယွန်းထည်
metal bowl	p'ălà	ဖလား
oboe	hnèh	နဲ

painting	băji-kà	ပန်းချီကား
plate	băgan	ပန်းကန်
ring	leq-suq	လက်စွပ်
shoulder bag	lweh-eiq	လွယ်အိတ်
small (pagoda) bell	s'wèh-lèh	ဆည်းလည်း
small cymbal-like bell	sì	စည်း
statue	youq-tú	ရုပ်တု
tray	lin-bàn/byaq	လင်ပန်း/ဗျပ်
umbrella	t'ì	ထီး
vase (for offerings to Buddha)	nyaun-ye-ò	ညောင်ရေအိုး
vase (for flowers)	pàn-ò	ပန်းအိုး
watercolour	ye-sè băji-kà	ရေဆေးပန်းချီကား

CLOTHING अण्णेऽाठाः

broad-brimmed bamboo hat (electoral symbol of NLD)	k'ǎmauq	ခမောက်
button	ceh-dhì	ကြယ်သီး
cloth	ǎt'eh	အထည်
clothing	ǎwuq-ǎsà	အဝတ်အစား
coat/jacket	taiq-poun	တိုက်ပုံ
cotton (pure)	c'i-deh siq-siq	ချည်ထည်စစ်စစ်
hat	ouq-t'ouq	ဦးထုပ်
longyi (sarong)		
for men	pǎs'ò	ပုဆိုး
for women	t'ǎmein	ထဘီ
shirt	eìn-ji	အကျႌ
shoelace	p'ǎnaq-cò	ဖိနပ်ကြိုး
shoes	p'ǎnaq	ဖိနပ်
silk	pò-deh	ပိုးထည်
thread	aq-c'i	အပ်ချည်
zipper	ziq	ဇစ်

Can I try it on?
wuq-cí-ló-yá-mǎlà?   ဝတ်ကြည့်လို့ရမလား။

It's too ...	ǎyàn ...	အရမ်း ...
big	cì-deh	ကြီးတယ်။
small	thè-deh	သေးတယ်။
short	to-deh	တိုတယ်။
long	sheh-deh	ရှည်တယ်။

MATERIALS

အဝတ်စ

amber	păyìn	ပယင်း
bronze/copper	cè-ni	ကြေးနီ
diamond	sein	စိန်
emerald	myá	မြ
gold (pure)	shwe (ăsiq)	ရွှေအစစ်
iron	than	သံ
jade	cauq-seìn	ကျောက်စိမ်း
	(lit: stone-green)	
ruby	bădămyà	ပတ္တမြား
silver (pure)	ngwe (ăsiq)	ငွေအစစ်
wood	thiq-thà	သစ်သား

COLOURS

အရောင်များ

colour	ăyaun	အရောင်
black	ămèh	အမဲ
blue	ăpya	အပြာ
brown	ănyo	အညို
green	ăsein	အစိမ်း
orange	lein-maw-yaun	လိမ္မော်ရောင်
pink	pàn-yaun	ပန်းရောင်
	(lit: flower-colour)	
purple	k'ăyàn-yaun	ခရမ်းရောင်
	(lit: eggplant-colour)	
red	ăni	အနီ
white	ăp'yu	အဖြူ
yellow	ăwa	အဝါ
a white hat	ouq-t'ouq-p'yu	ဦးထုပ်ဖြူ
a black umbrella	t'ì ămèh	ထီးအမဲ
three red books	sa-ouq-ni thoùn-ouq	စာအုပ်နီသုံးအုပ်

TOILETRIES

ရေချိုးခန်းသုံးပစ္စည်းများ

comb	bì	ဘီး
lipstick	hnăk'àn-ni	နှုတ်ခမ်းနီ
mirror	hman	မှန်
shampoo	gaùn-shaw-ye	ခေါင်းလျှော်ရည်
soap	s'aq-pya	ဆပ်ပြာ
toilet paper	ein-dha-thoùn-seq-ku	အိမ်သာသုံးစက္ကူ
toothbrush	dhăbuq-tan	သွားပွတ်တံ
toothpaste	thwà-taiq-s'è	သွားတိုက်ဆေး

STATIONERY & PUBLICATIONS

စာရေးကိရိယာနှင့် စာအုပ်စာတန်း

Is there an English-language
bookshop nearby?

   di-nà-hma   ဒီနားမှာ
   in-găleiq-săouq-s'ain shí-là?   အင်္ဂလိပ်စာအုပ်ဆိုင်ရှိလား။

Is there an English-language
section?

   ìn-găleiq-săouq-gan-dá shí-là?   အင်္ဂလိပ်စာအုပ်ကဏ္ဍ ရှိလား။

Do you sell ...?	... yaùn-là?	... ရောင်းလား။
magazines	meq-găzìn	မဂ္ဂဇင်း
newspapers	thădìn-sà	သတင်းစား
postcards	pó-săkaq	ပို့စကတ်

book	sa-ouq	စာအုပ်
dictionary	ăbí-dan	အဘိဓါန်
envelope	sa-eiq	စာအိတ်
guidebook	làn-hnyun	လမ်းညွှန်
map	mye-boun	မြေပုံ
notebook	hmaq-sú-sa-ouq	မှတ်စုစာအုပ်
paper	seq-ku	စက္ကူ
pen	bàw-pin	ဘောပင်
pencil	k'èh-dan	ခဲတံ

PHOTOGRAPHY ဓာတ်ပုံဆိုင်ရာ

I'd like a ...	... weh-jin-ba-deh	... ဝယ်ချင်ပါတယ်။
battery	daq-k'èh	ဓာတ်ခဲ
camera	kin-măra	ကင်မရာ
film	p'ălin	ဖလင်

SMOKING ဆေးလိပ်သောက်ခြင်း

No smoking.
s'è-leiq măthauq-yá ဆေးလိပ်မသောက်ရ

A packet of ...
... tăt'ouq ... တစ်ထုပ်

Excuse me, do you have a light?
k'ămyà/shin mì-jiq shí-là? (m/f) ခင်ဗျား/ရှင် မီးခြစ်ရှိလား။

Please don't smoke.
s'è-leiq măthauq-pa-néh ဆေးလိပ်မသောက်ပါနဲ့ ။

I'm trying to give up.
s'è-leiq-p'yaq-p'ó ဆေးလိပ်ဖြတ်ဖို့ကြီးစားနေတယ်။
cò-zà-ne-deh

Is it OK if I smoke?
s'è-leiq thauq-ló yá-mălà? ဆေးလိပ်သောက်လို့ ရမလား။

cheroot	s'è-bàw-leiq	ဆေးပေါလိပ်
cheroot (stronger)	s'è-byìn-leiq	ဆေးပြင်းလိပ်
cigarette	sì-găreq	စီးကရက်
matches	mì-jiq	မီးခြစ်

WEIGHTS & MEASURES

အလေးချိန်နှင့်အတိုင်းအတာ

Weights and measures are like counters (see Numbers & Amounts, page 153), in that they come after a number. When they are used, there is no need for a separate counter.

tical/kyat (16.5 g, 2/5 oz)	caq-thà	ကျပ်သား:
viss (1.65 kg, 3.65 lb)	peiq-tha	ပိဿာ
two viss of sugar	dhǎjà hnǎpeiq-tha	သကြား:နှစ်ပိဿာ
cup	k'weq	ခွက်
about two cups	hnǎk'weq-lauq	နှစ်ခွက်လောက်
inch	leq-má (lit: thumb)	လက်မ
foot	pe	ပေ
half yard	taun	တောင်
yard	gaiq	ကိုက်
mile	main	မိုင်
five miles	ngà-main	ငါ:မိုင်
acre	e-ká	ဧက

EGGSTRAVAGANT EARNINGS

Burmese people will have no qualms asking about your salary – it's a common topic of conversation. Whatever you earn, it will seem like a forture, unless you can put it into context. Convert the cost of an egg in your country into kyats. This is the best way to explain the cost of living where you come from.

SHOPPING

SIZES & COMPARISONS

အရွယ်နှင့် နှိုင်းယှဉ်ချက်

big	cì-deh	ကြီးတယ်
small	thè-deh	သေးတယ်
many	myà-deh	များတယ်
few	nèh-deh	နည်းတယ်
long	she-deh	ရှည်တယ်
short (length)	to-deh	တိုတယ်
high/tall	myín-deh	မြင့်တယ်
low/short (height)	neín-deh	နိမ့်တယ်
heavy	lè-deh	လေးတယ်
light	páw-deh	ပေါ့တယ်

FOOD

Most restaurants are privately run. Rice is the staple food and a full Burmese meal consists of a meat curry, some raw or cooked vegetables, a soup and rice – usually all served at once. The soup is eaten with a spoon, and everything else with the right hand. A snack could consist of a noodle dish or a curry. The food is not as overpoweringly hot as some Thai or Indian food, but chillies are used fairly liberally. Apart from Burmese food, various Shan dishes are popular. There are also good Chinese restaurants and Indian food stalls in most towns.

A very large variety of deep-fried or grilled vegetable and meat snacks are sold by street vendors during the day. There are also many different kinds of sweet snacks available, which are often eaten in the evening and at festivals. A number of delicious cold drinks are also available, as well as seasonal fruits.

THROUGH THE DAY   တစ်နေ့တာစားစရာ

breakfast	măneq-sa	မနက်စာ
lunch	né-leh-za	နေ့လယ်စာ
dinner	nyá-za	ညစာ
snack/small meal	moún/thăye-za	မုန့်/သရေစာ
food	sà-săya (lit: edibles)	စားစရာ
eat	sà-deh	စားတယ်
drink (v)	thauq-teh	သောက်တယ်

VEGETARIAN   သက်သတ်လွတ်နှင့် ၀ါတ်စာ
& SPECIAL DIETS

I'm a vegetarian.

     cănaw theq-thaq-luq-bèh   ကျွန်တော်သက်သတ်လွတ်ပဲ
     sà-deh (m)   စားတယ်။

I can't eat ...	... **măsà-nain-bù**	... မစားနိုင်ဘူး။
meat	**ăthà**	အသား
chillies	**ngăyouq-thì**	ငရုပ်သီး
peanuts	**mye-bèh**	မြေပဲ
(chicken) eggs	**ceq-ú**	ကြက်ဥ

I can't eat dairy products.
nó-t'weq-pyiq-sì măsà-bù နို့ထွက်ပစ္စည်းမစားဘူး။

Do you have any vegetarian dishes?
theq-thaq-luq-hìn shí-là? သက်သတ်လွတ်ဟင်း ရှိလား။

Does this dish have meat?
di hìn-hma thà pa-là? ဒီဟင်းမှာ သားပါလား။

EATING OUT စားသောက်ဆိုင်မှာစားခြင်း

Where is the restaurant?
sà-thauq-s'ain beh-hma-lèh? စားသောက်ဆိုင်ဘယ်မှာလဲ။

Is there a ... near here?	... **di-nà-hma shí-là?**	... ဒီနားမှာရှိလား။
Chinese restaurant	**tăyouq-s'ain**	တရုတ်ဆိုင်
Shan noodle stall	**shàn-k'auq-s'wèh-zain**	ရှမ်းခေါက်ဆွဲဆိုင်

What is there to eat?
ba sà-săya shí-dhălèh? ဘာစားစရာ ရှိသလဲ။

What is the best dish to eat today?
di-né ba-hìn ăkaùn-zoùn-lèh? ဒီနေ့ဘာဟင်းအကောင်းဆုံးလဲ။

(I/We) like spicy food.
saq-téh ăsa caiq-teh စပ်တဲ့အစာ ကြိုက်ပါယ်။

(I/We) don't eat spicy food.
ăsaq măsàbù အစပ် မစားဘူး။

Is it enough for three people?
thoùn-yauq sà-yin lauq-mălà? သုံးယောက်စားရင်လောက်မလား။

FOOD

(I am) hungry.
baiq-s'a-ne-deh ဗိုက်ဆာနေတယ်။

I didn't order this.
da măhma-t'à-bù ဒါ မမှာထားဘူး။

It is sweet.	c'o-deh	ချိုတယ်။
It is sour.	c'in-deh	ချဉ်တယ်။
It is spicy.	saq-teh	စပ်တယ်။
It is bitter.	k'à-deh	ခါးတယ်။

Please bring (a) ...	... pè-ba	... ပေးပါ။
bowl	băgan-loùn	ပန်းကန်လုံး
chopsticks	tu	တူ
cup	k'weq	ခွက်
fork	k'ăyìn	ခက်ရင်း
glass	p'an-gweq	ဖန်ခွက်
knife	dà	ဓါး
plate	băgan-byà	ပန်းကန်ပြား
spoon	zùn	ဇွန်း

Do you have (a) ...?	... shí-là?	... ရှိလား။
bigger table	po-jì-déh zăbwèh	ပိုကြီးတဲ့စားပွဲ
chair	kălăt'ain	ကုလားထိုင်
ice	ye-gèh	ရေခဲ

(I'd) like something to drink.
tăkú-gú thauq-c'in-deh တစ်ခုခု သောက်ချင်တယ်။

Do you have any drinking water?
thauq-ye shí-là? သောက်ရေရှိလား။

How much is it altogether?
à-loùn beh-lauq cá-lèh? အားလုံး ဘယ်လောက်ကျလဲ။

This is good to eat.
sà-ló kaùn-deh စားလို့ ကောင်းတယ်။

This is delicious.
di-ha ăya-dha theiq ဒီဟာ အရသာ သိပ်
kaùn-deh ကောင်းတယ်။

FOOD

MENU DECODER

SOUPS

အရည်ဟင်း

bèh-baun-hìn-jo	ဘဲပေါင်ဟင်းချို	duck soup
hìn-jo	ဟင်းချို	clear soup
hìn-nú-neh-hìn-jo	ဟင်းနုနယ်ဟင်းချို	green soup
moun-la-ú-hìn-jo	မုန်လာဥဟင်းချို	radish soup
s'an-hlaw-hìn-jo	ဆန်လှော်ဟင်းချို	sizzling rice soup
s'eh-hnǎmyò-hìn-jo	ဆယ်နှစ်မျိုးဟင်းချို	'12-taste' soup
yò-dǎyà-hìn-jo	ယိုးဒယားဟင်းချို	'Thai' soup (sour, like Thai tom yam)

NOODLES

ခေါက်ဆွဲ

Noodles (k'auq-s'wèh, ခေါက်ဆွဲ) of all shapes and sizes are a popular breakfast dish in Myanmar. Mohinga is almost the national dish. The ingredients in the sauce vary according to the cook and the area of Myanmar. Shan noodles are also popular and are sold at stalls throughout Myanmar. They tend to contain more tomatoes and less oil than mohinga, and may also contain meat.

ca-zan-hìn-gà	ကြာဆန်ဟင်းခါး	vermicelli with chicken
moún-di	မုန့်တီ	'Mandalay' moun-ti (spaghetti-like noodles with chicken or fish)
moún-hìn-gà	မုန့်ဟင်းခါး	mohinga (rice vermicelli in fish soup)
oùn-nó k'auq-swèh	အုန်းနို့ခေါက်ဆွဲ	coconut noodles (with chicken and egg)
shàn-k'auq-swèh	ရှမ်းခေါက်ဆွဲ	Shan noodles

RICE   ထမင်း

kauq-hnyìn	ကောက်ညှင်း	sticky rice
kauq-hnyìn-baùn	ကောက်ညှင်းပေါင်	packet/bamboo section of sticky rice
oùn-t'ămìn	အုန်းထမင်း	coconut rice
s'an	ဆန်	husked, uncooked rice
s'an-byouq	ဆန်ပြုတ်	rice gruel
shàn-t'ămìn-gyin	ရှမ်းထမင်းချဉ်	Shan sticky rice, meat and garlic packed in leaves and pickled
t'ămìn	ထမင်း	cooked rice
t'ămìn-gyaw	ထမင်းကြော်	fried rice

MEAT DISHES   အသားဟင်း

ămèh-dhà-hìn	အမဲသားဟင်း	beef curry
ămèh-hnaq	အမဲနပ်	beef in gravy
ăthà	အသား	meat
ceq-thà-ăc'o-jeq	ကြက်သားအချိုချက်	sweet chicken
ceq-thà-ăsaq-jeq	ကြက်သားအစပ်ချက်	fried spicy chicken
ceq-thà-gin	ကြက်သားကင်	grilled chicken (satay)
ceq-thà-hìn	ကြက်သားဟင်း	chicken curry
ceq-thà-jaw	ကြက်သားကြော်	fried chicken
weq-thà-hìn	ဝက်သားဟင်း	pork curry
weq-thà-ni	ဝက်သားနီ	red pork
weq-thà s'i-byan	ဝက်သားဆီပြန်	pork curry in thick sauce

FOOD

FOOD

SEAFOOD

ပင်လယ်ဟင်း

băzun-hìn	ပုစွန်ဟင်း	shrimp/prawn curry
băzun-thouq	ပုစွန်သုပ်	prawn salad
k'ăyú	ခရု	shellfish
ngà	ငါး	fish
ngà-baùn	ငါးပေါင်း	steamed fish
ngà-baùn-douq	ငါးပေါင်းထုပ်	steamed fish in banana leaves
ngà-dhouq	ငါးသုပ်	fish salad
ngăk'u	ငါးခူ	catfish
ngămyìn	ငါးမြင်း	butterfish
ngăshín	ငါးရှဉ့်	eel
ngà-thălauq-paùn	ငါးသလောက်ပေါင်း	steamed carp
pin-leh-za/ ye-thaq-tăwa	ပင်လယ်စာ/ ရေသတ္တဝါ	seafood
pyi-ji-ngà	ပြည်ကြီးငါး	squid

EGGS

၉

bèh-ú	ဘဲဥ	duck egg
ceq-ú	ကြက်ဥ	chicken egg
ceq-ú-byouq	ကြက်ဥပြုတ်	boiled (chicken) egg
ceq-ú-ceq-thun-jaw	ကြက်ဥကြက်သွန်ကြော်	omelette (with onions)
ceq-ú-jaw	ကြက်ဥကြော်	fried (chicken) egg

FOOD

FOREIGN FOODS   နိုင်ငံခြားအစားအစာ

dan-bauq	ဒန်ပေါက်	biryani (rice with meat and spices, an Indian dish)
kaw-pyán-jaw	ကော်ပြန့်ကြော်	spring rolls/egg rolls
paun-moún	ပေါင်မုန့်	bread
paun-moún-gin	ပေါင်မုန့်ကင်	toast
to-she	တိုရှေ	dosa (potato-filled pancake, South Indian)

SAUCES & CONDIMENTS   အချဉ်နှင့်ဟင်းခတ်အမွှေးအကြိုင်

jìn-dhouq	ဂျင်းသုပ်	ginger salad
kǎlǎt'àw-baq	ကုလားထောပတ်	ghee
kùn-yà	ကွမ်းယား	betel quid
lǎp'eq	လက်ဖက်	pickled green tea
mye-bèh	မြေပဲ	peanuts
mye-bèh-jaw	မြေပဲကြော်	fried peanuts
ngan-pya-ye	ငံပြာရည်	fish sauce
ngǎpí	ငါးပိ	fish/prawn paste
ngǎpí-gaun	ငါးပိကောင်	whole salted fish
ngǎpí-seìn-zà	ငါးပိစိမ်းစား	raw prawn fish paste
ngǎpí-ye	ငါးပိရည်	fish paste sauce
ngǎpyàw-jaw	ငှက်ပျောကြော်	fried bananas
ngǎyouq-ye	ငရုတ်ရည်	chilli sauce
oùn-nó	အုန်းနို့	coconut cream
pǎyiq-caw	ပုရစ်ကြော်	fried cicadas
pèh-ngan-pya-ye	ပဲငံပြာရည်	soy sauce
pyà-ye	ပျားရည်	honey

FOOD

s'à	ဆား	salt
sha-lăka-ye	ရှာလကာရည်	vinegar
t'àw-baq	ထောပတ်	butter
tha-gu	သာဂူ	sago/tapioca
thăjà	သကြား	sugar
thi-ho-zí	သီဟိုစေ့	cashews
to-hù	တိုဟူး	tofu/beancurd
to-hù-c'auq	တိုဟူးခြောက်	tofu crackers
to-hù-jaw	တိုဟူးကြော်	fried tofu squares
to-hù-pyáw	တိုဟူးပျော့	tofu porridge
t'oùn	ထုံး	lime (for betel)
zăbyiq-thì-jauq	စပျစ်သီးခြောက်	raisins

SWEETS & CAKES   အချိုနှင့်ကိတ်မုန့်

When you sit down in a teashop, the waiter will usually bring you a selection of snacks without being asked. Don't worry – you will only be charged for what you eat.

bí-săkiq-moún	ဘစ်စကစ်မုန့်	biscuit/cookie
cauq-càw	ကျောက်ကျော	agar-agar (bright green or cream-coloured jelly sweet, can be drunk in a liquid)
dhăjà-loùn	သကြားလုံး	sugar candy
dù-yìn-yo	ဒူးရင်းယို	durian cooked in jaggery
i-ca-kwè	အီကြာကွေး	deep-fried dough-sticks (like Chinese 'you zha gui')
kauq-hnyìn-baùn	ကောက်ညှင်းပေါင်း	steamed sticky rice
kauq-hnyìn-ngăjeiq	ကောက်ညှင်းချို	sticky rice cake (purple)

FOOD

keiq-moún	ကိတ်မုန့်	cake
moún-ceq-ú	မုန့်ကြက်အု	sticky rice cake with jaggery and egg
moún-jaw	မုန့်ကြော်	fried cake/snack
moún-le-bwe	မုန့်လေပေ	sticky rice wafer
moún-leq-s'aùn	မုန့်လက်ဆောင်း	jaggery, coconut milk and rice jelly (solid or drink)
moún-lin-mǎyà	မုန့်လင်မယား	'husband & wife sweet' (hot circular rice sweet)
moún-ò-hnauq (lit: brain sweet)	မုန့်ဦးနှောက	steamed rice dough pudding
moún-sein-baùn	မုန့်စိမ်းပေါင်း	steamed cake with shredded coconut
moún-s'i-jaw	မုန့်ဆီကြော်	sweet fried rice pancakes
moún-zàn	မုန့်ဆန်း	sticky rice cake with jaggery
s'ǎnwìn-mǎkìn	ဆန္နင်းမကင်း	semolina pudding
shwe-t'ǎmìn	ရွှေထမင်	golden rice (sticky)
t'àn-thì-moún	ထန်းသီးမုန့်	toddy palm sugar cake
t'ǎnyeq	ထန်းလျက်	jaggery (toddy candy)
t'ǎmǎnèh	ထမနဲ့	sticky rice pudding with sesamum (for Tabaung new moon)
tha-gu-moún	သာဂူမုန့်	sago/tapioca in syrup
ye-gèh-moún	ရေခဲမုန့်	ice cream
zì-yo	ဆီးယို	jujube plums cooked in jaggery

FOOD

VEGETABLES   ဟင်းသီးဟင်းရွက်

vegetables	hìn-dhì-hìn-yweq	ဟင်းသီးဟင်းရွက်
banana flower	ngăpyàw-bù	ငှက်ပျောဖူး
beans	pèh-dhì	ပဲသီး
cabbage	gaw-bi-douq	ဂေါ်ဖီထုပ်
carrot	moun-la-ú-wa	မုန့်လာဥဝါ
cauliflower	pàn-gaw-bi	ပန်းဂေါ်ဖီ
chickpeas	kălăbèh	ကုလားပဲ
corn (cob)	pyaùn-bù	ပြောင်းဖူး
cucumber	thăk'wà-dhì	သခွါးသီး
eggplant/ aubergine	k'ăyàn-dhì	ခရမ်းသီး
fried vegetables	hìn-dhì-hìn-yweq-caw	ဟင်းသီးဟင်းရွက်ကြော်
green beans	pèh-daún-she	ပဲတောင့်ရှည်
lettuce	s'ălaq-yweq	ဆလတ်ရွက်
mushrooms	hmo	မှို
onion	ceq-thun-ni	ကြက်သွန်နီ
pickled salad	thănaq	သနပ်
pumpkin	p'ăyoun-dhì	ဖရုံသီး
salad	ăthouq	အသုပ်
tomato	k'ăyàn-jin-dhì	ခရမ်းချဉ်သီး
white radish	moun-la-ú-p'yu	မုန့်လာဥဖြူ
vegetable curry	hìn-dhì-hìn-yweq-hìn/ thì-soun-hìn	ဟင်းသီးဟင်းရွက်ဟင်း/ သီးစုံဟင်း
zucchini/gourd	bù-dhì	ဘူးသီး

GETTING YOUR EAR AROUND IT

'I understand' is nà-leh-ba-deh;
'I don't understand' is nà-mă-leh-ba-bù.
It literally means 'I can/can't get my ear around it'.

FRUIT

အသီးအနှံ

fruit	thiq-thì	သစ်သီး
apple	pàn-dhì	ပန်းသီး
	(lit: flower-fruit)	
avocado	t'àw-baq-thì	ထောပတ်သီး
	(lit: butter-fruit)	
banana	ngăpyàw-dhì	ငှက်ပျောသီး
breadfruit	paun-moún-dhì	ပေါင်မုန့်သီး
coconut	oùn-dhì	အုန်းသီး
custard apple	àw-za-thì	ဩဇာသီး
	(lit: influence-fruit)	
durian	dù-yìn-dhì	ဒူးရင်းသီး
lemon	shauq-thì	ရှောက်သီး
lime	than-băya-dhì	သံပုရာသီး
lychee	lain-c'ì-dhì	လိုင်ချီးသီး

FOOD

mango	thăyeq-dhì	သရက်သီး
orange	lein-maw-dhì	လိမ္မော်သီး
papaya	thìn-bàw-dhì	သင်္ဘောသီး
	(lit: boat-shaped fruit)	
peach	meq-mun-dhì	မက်မွန်သီး
pear	thiq-taw-dhì	သစ်တော်သီး
pineapple	na-naq-thì	နာနတ်သီး
plum (damson)	meq-màn-dhì	မက်မန်းသီး
jujube plum	zì-dhì	ဆီးသီး
pomelo	cwèh-gàw-dhì	ကျွဲကောသီး
rambutan	ceq-mauq-thì	ကြက်မောက်သီး
	(lit: cockscomb fruit)	
tamarind	măji-dhì	မန်ကျည်းသီး
watermelon	p'ăyèh-dhì	ပရဲသီး

FOOD

HERBS & SPICES   ဟင်းခတ်ပင်နှင့်အမွှေးအကြိုင်

cardamon	p'a-la-zí	ဖါလာစေ့
chilli	ngăyouq-thì	ငရုတ်သီး
coriander	nan-nan-bin	နံနံပင်
galangal (white ginger-like root)	meiq-thălin	မိတ်သလင်
garlic	ceq-thun-byu	ကြက်သွန်ဖြူ
ginger	gyìn	ဂျင်း
lemongrass	zăbălin	စပါးလင်
rose syrup	hnìn-yi	နှင်းရည်
sesame	hnàn	နှမ်း
turmeric	s'ănwìn	ဆနွင်း

DRINKS   သောက်စရာ
Cold Drinks   အအေး

coconut juice	oùn-ye	အုန်းရည်
lime juice	than-băya-ye	သံပရာရည်
milk	nwà-nó	နွားနို့
orange juice	lein-maw-ye	လိမ္မော်ရည်
soft drink	bí-laq-ye/p'yaw-ye	ဘီလပ်ရည်/ဖျော်ရည်
sugarcane juice	can-ye	ကြံရည်
water	ye	ရေ
bottled water	ye-thán	ရေသန့်
cold water	ye-è	ရေအေး
hot water	ye-nwè	ရေနွေး
soda water	s'o-da	ဆိုဒါ

Hot Drinks

အပူ

Plain green, Chinese (or Shan) tea is free in all restaurants and teashops and a thermos of it sits on the table of most Burmese homes. Coffee and other types of tea tend to come pre-mixed in the cup with milk (or condensed milk) and plenty of sugar. If you ask for a black coffee, you may get local coffee (delicious black with a wedge of lime) or instant coffee, known as **Nes**. Sachets of 'coffee-mix' (coffee, milk powder and sugar) are becoming widespread.

Please don't add ...	... măt'éh-ba-néh	... မထဲ့ပါနဲ့
condensed milk	nó-zì	နို့ဆီ
sugar	dhăjà	သကြား
coffee	kaw-fi	ကော်ဖီ
plain green tea	lăp'eq-ye-jàn/	လက်ဖက်ရည်ကြမ်း/
	ye-nwè-jàn	ရေနွေးကြမ်း
Indian tea	leq-p'eq-ye	လက်ဖက်ရည်
with milk	nwà-nó-néh	နွားနို့နဲ့
with condensed milk	nó-zì-néh	နို့ဆီနဲ့
with lime	than-băya-dhì-néh	သံပရာသီးနဲ့
with sugar	dhăjà-néh	သကြားနဲ့
one bottle	dăbălìn	တစ်ပုလင်း
two cups	hnăk'weq	နှစ်ခွက်

BURMESE HOSPITALITY

The best cuisine in Myanmar is home cooking. If you are lucky enough to be invited to eat in someone's home, don't be put off if most of the family have eaten before you arrive and instead prefer to watch you eat on your own. The women of the family may even prefer to hang out in the kitchen, only emerging to fill your plate.

FOOD

Alcoholic Drinks

အရက်ပါသောသောက်စရာ

Please bring two bottles of beer.
  bi-ya hnăbălìn pè-ba

ဘီယာနှစ်ပုလင်းပေးပါ။

a bottle/glass of ...	tăbălìn/tăk'weq ...	တစ်ပုလင်း/တစ်ခွက် ...
red wine	wain-ăni	ဝိုင်အနီ
white wine	wain-ăp'yu	ဝိုင်အဖြူ

a ... of beer	bi-ya ...	ဘီယာ ...
small bottle	tăbălìn-thè	တစ်ပုလင်းသေး
large bottle	tăbălìn-jì	တစ်ပုလင်းကြီး

alcohol	ăyeq	အရက်
beer	bi-ya	ဘီယာ
toddy	t'àn-yi	ထန်းရည်
wine	wain	ဝိုင်

IN THE COUNTRY

While it is quite safe to walk in all towns, walking in the countryside may be unwise, especially in the former grey (rebel-contested) or black (rebel-controlled) areas. Although nearly all the ethnic rebellions have been ended by truces, most of the former ethnic rebels are still in place – with their weapons and a considerable distrust of outsiders – and in some remote areas there is still fighting.

ETHNIC MINORITIES   တိုင်းရင်းသားလူမျိုးစုများ

The country is divided into seven divisions (taìn, တိုင်း), which are in the centre of the country, and seven states (pye-neh, ပြည်နယ်), which are around the borders. Each state is designated according to the largest minority group living there. These minorities are as follows:

Rakhine (Arakanese)	răk'ain	ရခိုင်
Chin	c'ìn	ချင်း
Kachin	kăc'in	ကချင်
Shan	shàn	ရှမ်း
Kayah (Karenni)	kăyà	ကယား
Karen	kăyin	ကရင်
Mon	mun	မွန်
national minority	taìn-yìn-dhà-lu-myò	တိုင်းရင်းသားလူမျိုး

There are more than a hundred other minorities, many of whom live in the Shan, Chin and Kachin States. Many of these minority groups are also found in China, Thailand, Laos, India and Bangladesh.

HIKING — ခြေလျင်လျှောက်ခြင်း

Getting Information — အချက်အလက်ရယူခြင်း

Who can I ask about hiking trails in the region?
: **di-nà-hma làn-shauq-leh-bó bădhú-go mè-yá-mălèh?** — ဒီနားမှာ လမ်းလျှောက်လည်ဖို့ ဘယ်သူ့ကို မေးရမလဲ။

Where's the nearest village?
: **ănì-zoùn-ywa beh-nà-hma-lèh?** — အနီးဆုံးရွာ ဘယ်နားမှာလဲ။

Do we need a guide?
: **gaiq ngà-da ălo-shî-là?** — ဂိုက်ငှားတာ အလိုရှိလား။

Is the track easy to follow?
: **làn-shauq-leh-bó lweh-là?** — လမ်းလျှောက်လည်ဖို့ လွယ်လား။

How high is the climb?
: **beh-lauq myín-myín teq-yá-mălèh?** — ဘယ်လောက်မြင့်မြင့် တက်ရမလဲ။

Which is the shortest route?
: **beh làn ăto-zoùn-lèh?** — ဘယ်လမ်းအတိုဆုံးလဲ။

Which is the easiest route?
: **beh làn ălweh-zoùn-lèh?** — ဘယ်လမ်းအလွယ်ဆုံးလဲ။

Is the path open?
: **làn pwín-t'à-là?** — လမ်းဖွင့်ထားလား။

When does it get dark?
: **beh ăc'ein hmaun-mălèh?** — ဘယ်အချိန်မှောင်မလဲ။

On the Path — လမ်းပေါ်မှာ

Please show me the way to ...
: **... ko làn pyá-pè-ba** — ... ကို လမ်းပြပေးပါ။

How far is it to ...?
: **... ko beh-lauq-wè-dhălèh?** — ... ကို ဘယ်လောက်ဝေးသလဲ။

How many hours will it take?
: **beh-lauq ca-ja thwà-yá-mălèh?** — ဘယ်လောက် ကြာကြာသွားရမလဲ။

Are there any road signs?
    làn-ăhmaq-ăthà shí-là?   လမ်းအမှတ်အသား ရှိလား။

Are there street signs/names?
    làn-na-meh yè-t'à-dhălà?   လမ်းနာမယ် ရေးထားသလား။

Which way?
    beh-làn-lèh?   ဘယ်လမ်းလဲ။

I don't think this is the right way.
    di-làn măhman-bù t'in-deh   ဒီလမ်းမမှန်ဘူး ထင်တယ်။

(I'm/We're) lost.
    làn pyauq-thwà-bi   လမ်းပျောက်သွားပြီ။

Where can we spend the night?
    nyá beh-hma nà-nain-mălèh?   ည ဘယ်မှာနားနိုင်မလဲ။

Please turn back.
    pyan-hléh-ba   ပြန်လှည့်ပါ။

Is the water OK to drink?
    di ye thauq-ló yá-là?   ဒီရေ သောက်လို့ရလား။

IN THE COUNTRY

IN THE COUNTRY

altitude	pin-leh-ye myeq-hnǎbyin-hmá ǎmyín	ပင်လယ်ရေမျက်နှာပြင်မှ အမြင့်
backpack	càw-bò-eiq	ကျောပိုးအိတ်
binoculars	ǎwè-jí hman-pyàun	အဝေးကြည့် မှန်ပြောင်း
candles	p'ǎyaùn-dain	ဖယောင်းတိုင်
climb	teq-deh	တက်တယ်
compass	than-laiq-ein-hmaun	သံလိုက်အိမ်မြောင်
downhill	ǎs'in-beq-ko	အဆင်းဘက်ကို
first-aid kit	shè-ú-thu-na-byú thiq-ta	ရှေးဦးသူနာပြုသေတ္တာ
gloves	leq-eiq	လက်အိတ်
guide	gaiq	ဂိုက်
hiking	c'e-lyin k'ǎyì t'weq-ta	ခြေလျင်ခရီးထွက်တာ
hiking boots	k'ǎyì-jàn p'ǎnaq	ခရီးကြမ်းဖိနပ်
hunting	ǎmèh laiq-ta	အမဲလိုက်တာ
ledge	cauq-sùn	ကျောက်စွန်း
lookout	shú-gìn-tha	ရှုခင်းသာ
map	mye-boun	မြေပုံ
provisions	làn-ǎtweq ǎsà-ǎsa	လမ်းအတွက်အစားအစာ
signpost	s'àin-bouq	ဆိုင်းဘုတ်
steep	maq-sauq-teh	မတ်စောက်တယ်
trek	trek	ထရက်
uphill	ǎt'eq-ko	အထက်ကို
walk (v)	làn shauq	လမ်းလျှောက်

MEETING & GREETING

In formal situations and in cities, greet people with min-gǎla-ba, literally 'It's a blessing'. For any informal encounter, 'Are you well?', ne-kaùn-yéh-là? is fine . You can reply with ne-kaùn-ba-deh, 'I am well'.

AT THE BEACH

ပင်လယ်ကမ်းခြေတွင်

Can we swim here?
di-hma ye-kù-ló yá-mălà?
ဒီမှာရေကူးလို့ရမလား။

Is there a (public) beach near here?
di-nà-hma pin-leh-kàn-je shí-là?
ဒီနားမှာ ပင်လယ်ကမ်းခြေ ရှိလား။

coast	kàn-yò-dàn	ကမ်းရိုးတန်း
coral	than-da cauq	သန္တာကျောက်
beach	kàn-byin	ကမ်းပြင်
lagoon	pin-leh-kàn-je-ain	ပင်လယ်ကမ်းခြေအိုင်
ocean	thămouq-dăya	သမုဒ္ဒရာ
reef	cauq-tàn	ကျောက်တန်း
rock	cauq	ကျောက်
sand	thèh	သဲ
sea	pin-leh	ပင်လယ်
snorkelling	le-bun-byín ye-ngouq-ta	လေပြွန်ဖြင့်ရေငုပ်တာ
sunblock	ne-laun-jìn-hmá ka-gweh-zè	နေလောင်ခြင်းမှ ကာကွယ်ဆေး
sunglasses	ne-ka myeq-hman	နေကာမျက်မှန်
surf	ye-hlaìn	ရေလှိုင်း
swimming	ye kù-da	ရေကူးတာ
towel	myeq-hnăthouq-păwa	မျက်နှာသုတ်ပုဝါ
waves	hlaìn	လှိုင်း

IN THE COUNTRY

Aquatic Creatures

ရေသတ္တဝါ

crab	gănàn	ဂဏန်း
dolphin	lìn-bain	လင်းပိုင်
fish	ngà	ငါး
shark	ngămàn	ငါးမန်း
shrimp/ prawn	băzun	ပုဇွန်
turtle	leiq	လိပ်

WEATHER ရာသီ ဥတု

cool season (October to January)	s'aùn-ya-dhi	ဆောင်းရာသီ
hot season (February to May)	nwe-ya-dhi	နွေရာသီ
rainy season (June to September)	mò-dwìn	မိုးတွင်း

cloud	tein	တိမ်
fog	hnìn	နှင်း
monsoon	mò-theq-le-pyìn	မိုးသက်လေပြင်း
rain (v)	mò-ywa-deh	မိုးရွာတယ်
season	ya-dhi-ú-dú	ရာသီဥတု
weather	mò-le-wădhá	မိုးလေဝသ
wind	le	လေ

What will the weather be like today?
 di-né mò-le-wădhá beh-lo-lèh? ဒီနေ့ မိုးလေဝသ ဘယ်လိုလဲ။

The weather is ...	mò-le-wădhá ...	မိုးလေဝသ ...
good	kaùn-deh	ကောင်းတယ်။
changeable	pyaùn-nain-deh	ပြောင်းနိုင်တယ်။
bad	s'ò-deh	ဆိုးတယ်။

It is very hot today.
 di-né theiq pu-deh ဒီနေ့ သိပ်ပူတယ်။
Will it rain tomorrow?
 măneq-p'yan mò-ywa-mălà? မနက်ဖြန် မိုးရွာမလား။
There is no wind.
 le-mătaiq-p'ù လေမတိုက်ဘူး။
Are you cold?
 k'ămyà/shin theiq c'àn-ne-là? (m/f) ခင်ဗျား/ရှင် သိပ်ချမ်းနေလား။
The rain has stopped.
 mò-teiq-pi မိုးတိတ်ပြီ။

PLACE NAMES   နေရာဒေသနာမည်းများ
Main Towns   မြို့.မများ

Yangon (Rangoon)	yan-goun	ရန်ကုန်
Mandalay	màn-dǎlè	မန္တလေး
Bagan (Pagan)	bǎgan	ပုဂံ
Taunggyi	taun-jì	တောင်ကြီး

Towns Around Yangon (Rangoon)   ရန်ကုန်အနီးရှိမြို့များ

Syriam	tǎnyin	သံလျင်
Bago (Pegu)	bǎgò	ပဲခူး
Mawlamyaing (Moulmein)	maw-lǎmyain	မော်လမြိုင်
Pyay (Prome)	pye	ပြည်

Towns Around Mandalay   မန္တလေးအနီးရှိမြို့များ

Sagaing	zǎgàin	စစ်ကိုင်း
Mingun	mìn-gùn	မင်းကွန်း
Pyin-Oo-Lwin (Maymyo)	pyin-ù-lwin (me-myó)	ပြင်ဦးလွင် (မေမြို့.)

Towns Around Bagan (Pagan)   ပုဂံအနီးရှိမြို့များ

Nyaung-oo	nyaun-ù	ညောင်ဦး
Kyaukpadaung	cauq-pǎdàun	ကျောက်ပန်းတောင်း

Towns Around Taunggyi   တောင်ကြီးအနီးရှိမြို့များ

Heho	hèh-hò	ဟဲဟိုး
Shwenyaung	shwe-nyaun	ရွှေညောင်
Inle Lake	ìn-lè-kan	အင်းလေးကန်

IN THE COUNTRY

Further Afield   ပိုဝေးသောနေရာများ:

Dawei (Tavoy)	däweh	ထားဝယ်
Myeik (Mergui)	beiq	မြိတ်
Lashio	là-shò	လားရှိုး
Kengtung (Kyaingtong)	caìn-toun	ကျိုင်းတုံ
Thandwe	than-dwèh	သံတွဲ
(Sandoway beach resort)		
Sittwe (Akyab)	sit-twe	စစ်တွေ
Pathein (Bassein)	päthein	ပုသိမ်
Bhamo	bämaw	ဗန်းမော်
Myitkyina	myit-cì-nà	မြစ်ကြီးနား

Rivers   မြစ်များ:

Ayeyarwady (Irrawaddy)	e-ya-wá-di	ဧရာဝတီ
Chindwin	c'ìn-dwìn	ချင်းတွင်း
Thanlwin (Salween)	than-lwin	သံလွင်

GEOGRAPHICAL TERMS   ပထဝီဆိုင်ရာအသုံးအနှုန်း:

countryside	tàw	တော
field (irrigated)	leh	လယ်
hill	taun/koùn	တောင်/ကုန်း
island	cùn	ကျွန်း
lake	ain	အိုင်
lake (small/artificial)	kan	ကန်
map	mye-boun	မြေပုံ
mountain	taun	တောင်
river	myiq	မြစ်
sandbank	thaun	သောင်
town	myó	မြို့
track/trail	làn-jaùn	လမ်းကြောင်း
village	ywa	ရွာ
waterfall	ye-dägun	ရေတံခွန်

FAUNA

တိရစ္ဆာန်များ

What animal is that?

da ba dăreiq-s'an lèh?

ဒါဘာ တိရစ္ဆာန် လဲ။

bedbug	jăbò	ကြမ်းပိုး
bee	pyà	ပျား
bird	hngeq	ငှက်
buffalo	cwèh	ကျွဲ
butterfly	leiq-pya	လိပ်ပြာ
cat	caun	ကြောင်
chicken	ceq	ကြက်
cow	nwà	နွား
deer (barking)	ji	ချေ
deer (sambhar)	s'aq	ဆတ်
dog	k'wè	ခွေး

duck	bèh	ဘဲ
elephant	s'in	ဆင်
fly	yin-gaun	ယင်ကောင်
frog	p'à	ဖါး
gecko	tauq-téh	တောက်တဲ့
goat	s'eiq	ဆိတ်
horse	myìn	မြင်း
insect	pò-gaun	ပိုးကောင်
lizard	p'uq	ဖွတ်
mosquito	c'in	ခြင်
pig	weq	ဝက်
rat	cweq	ကြွက်
snake	mwe	မြွေ
tiger	cà	ကျား

FLORA

အပင်နှင့်သစ်ပင်များ

What ... is that?	da ba ... lèh?	ဒါဘာ ... လဲ။
flower	pàn-pin	ပန်းပင်
tree	thiq-pin	သစ်ပင်

What plant is that?
da ba ăpin-lèh? ဒါ ဘာအပင်လဲ။

Please could you write down the name for me?
na-meh yè-pè-ba? နာမယ်ရေးပေးပါ။

bamboo	wà	ဝါး
bark	thiq-k'auq	သစ်ခေါက်
flower	pàn	ပန်း
flowering plant	pàn-bin	ပန်းပင်
leaf	thiq-yweq	သစ်ရွက်
lotus	ca	ကြာ
orchid	thiq-k'wá-pàn	သစ်ခွပန်း
pine	t'ìn-yù-bin	ထင်းရှူးပင်
rattan	cein	ကြိမ်
teak	cùn-thiq	ကျွန်းသစ်
tree	thiq-pin	သစ်ပင်
wood	thiq-thà	သစ်သား

HEALTH

Foreign residents of Myanmar who become seriously ill usually go overseas for treatment. However, if you do need some kind of medical treatment this chapter should be useful. Be aware that the incidence of infectious diseases is high, the standard of public hospitals is very low and almost no medicines or other supplies are available from hospitals or government shops – generally, even the most basic medicines must be bought 'outside' (ăpyin, အပြင်) on the private market.

Where is the ...?	... beh-hma-lèh?	... ဘယ်မှာလဲ။
ambulance	lu-na-tin-yin	လူနာတင်ယာဉ်
doctor	s'ăya-wun	ဆရာဝန်
dentist	thwà-s'ăya-wun	သွားဆရာဝန်
hospital	s'è-youn	ဆေးရုံ
medical super-intendent (chief doctor of hospital)	s'è-youn-ouq	ဆေးရုံအုပ်
nurse	thu-na-byú	သူနာပြု
patient	lu-na	လူနာ
pharmacy/chemist	s'è-zain	ဆေးဆိုင်
private clinic	ăt'ù-gú-s'è-gàn	အထူးကုဆေးခန်း
specialist	ăt'ù-gú s'ăya-wun	အထူးကုဆရာဝန်

Please call a doctor.
s'ăya-wun k'aw-pè-ba ဆရာဝန် ခေါ်ပေးပါ။

AT THE DOCTOR   ဆရာဝန်ဆီမှာ

I need a doctor who speaks English.
ìn-găleiq-zăgà
pyàw-daq-téh săya-wun shí-là   အင်္ဂလိပ်စကား
                                       ပြောတတ်တဲ့ဆရာဝန် ရှိလား။

I'm not feeling very well.
theiq ne-măkaùn-bù   သိပ် နေမကောင်းဘူး။

Is it serious?; Should I be worried?
sò-yein-yá-dhălà?   စိုးရိမ်ရသလား။

I don't want an injection.
s'è măt'ò-ze-jin-ba-bù   ဆေး မထိုးစေချင်ပါဘူး။

I am allergic to penicillin.
cănaw/cămá pănăsălin-néh
mătéh-bù (m/f)   ကျွန်တော်/ ကျွန်မ
                                       ပင်နီစလင်နဲ့ မတည့်ဘူး။

My friend is sick.
cănáw thăngeh-jìn
ne-măkaùn-bù (m)   ကျွန်တော့် သူငယ်ချင်း
                                       နေမကောင်းဘူး။

I'm sick.	ne-măkaùn-bù	နေမကောင်းဘူး။
I feel tired.	pin-bàn-ne-bi	ပင်ပန်းနေပြီ။
I feel faint.	mù-lèh-deh	မူးလဲတယ်။
I vomit often.	k'ăná-k'ăná an-deh	ခဏခဏ အန်တယ်။
It hurts here.	di-hma na-deh	ဒီမှာ နာတယ်။
It itches here.	di-hma yà-deh	ဒီမှာ ယားတယ်။
I can't sleep.	eiq-mă-pyaw-bù	အိပ်မပျော်ဘူး။

addiction	s'è-zwèh-jìn	ဆေးစွဲခြင်း
bite	kaiq-ya	ကိုက်ရာ
blood test	thwè-siq	သွေးစစ်
diabetes	s'ì-jo-yàw-ga	ဆီးချိုရောဂါ
hypertension	thwè-do-yàw-ga	သွေးတိုးရောဂါ
inhaler	shú-zè	ရှူဆေး
injection	t'ò-zè	ထိုးဆေး
injury	t'í-k'aiq-dan-ya	ထိခိုက်ဒဏ်ရာ
insulin	in-s'u-lin	အင်ဆူလင်
penicillin	pănăsălin	ပင်နီစလင်

HEALTH

THEY MAY SAY ...

ba p'yiq-ta-lèh? ဘာ ဖြစ်တာလဲ။
What's the matter?

aún-dhǎlà? အောင့်သလား။
Do you feel any pain?

beh-hma na-dhèlèh? ဘယ်မှာ နာသလဲ။
Where does it hurt?

ya-dhi la-ne-là? ရာသီလာနေလား။
Are you menstruating?

ko-pu-jein shí-là? ကိုယ်ပူချိန်ရှိလား။
Do you have a temperature?

di-lo p'yiq-ne-da ဒီလိုဖြစ်နေတာ
beh-lauq-ca-bi-lèh? ဘယ်လောက်ကြာပြီလဲ။
How long have you been
like this?

di-lo ǎyin p'yiq-p'ù-là? ဒီလိုအရင်ဖြစ်ဖူးလား။
Have you had this before?

s'è thauq-ne-doùn-là? ဆေးသောက်နေတုန်းလား။
Are you on medication?

s'è-leiq thauq-là? ဆေးလိပ်သောက်လား။
Do you smoke?

ǎyeq thauq-là? အရက်သောက်လား။
Do you drink?

mù-yiq-s'è-wà thoùn-là? မူးယစ်ဆေးဝါးသုံးလား။
Do you take drugs?

mǎtéh-déh s'è shí-là? မတည့်တဲ့ဆေးရှိလား။
Are you allergic to anything?

ko-wun shí-là? ကိုယ်ဝန်ရှိလား။
Are you pregnant?

AILMENTS   ရောဂါများ

I/You have ...	... shí-deh/	... ရှိတယ်။
	... p'yiq-ne-deh	... ဖြစ်နေတယ်။
AIDS	A.I.D.S.-yàw-ga	အေအိုင်ဒီအက်စ်ရောဂါ
asthma	(pàn-na-)yin-caq	ပန်းနာရင်ကျပ်
cholera	ka-lá-wùn-yàw-ga	ကာလဝမ်းရောဂါ
dengue fever	thwè-lun-touq-kwè	သွေးလွန်တုပ်ကွေး
flu	touq-kwè	တုပ်ကွေး
hepatitis	ăthèh-yaun-yàw-ga	အသည်းရောင်ရောဂါ
malaria	hngeq-p'yà	ငှက်ဖျား
	(lit: bird-fever)	
rabies	k'wè-yù-byan-yàw-ga	ခွေးရူးပြန်ရောဂါ
venereal disease	ka-lá-dhà yàw-ga	ကာလသားရောဂါ

The following are expressed by adjectival verbs so you can use them on their own without shí-deh and p'yiq-ne-deh.

have anaemia	thwè-à nèh-deh	သွေးအားနည်းတယ်
have chest pain	yin-baq	ရင်ဘတ်
	aún-ne-deh	အောင့်နေတယ်။
have a cold	ăè mí-bi	အအေးမိပြီ
have a cough	c'aùn s'ò-deh	ချောင်းဆိုးတယ်
have cramps	cweq teq-teh	ကြွက်တက်တယ်
have diarrhoea	wùn-shàw-deh/	ဝမ်းလျှောတယ်/
	wùn-thwà-ne-deh	ဝမ်းသွားနေတယ်
have dysentery	wùn kaiq-ne-deh	ဝမ်းကိုက်နေတယ်
have a fever	p'yà-deh	ဖျားတယ်
have gonorrhea	găno cá-deh	ဂနိုကျတယ်
have a headache	gaùn kaiq-ne-deh	ခေါင်းကိုက်နေတယ်
have pneumonia	ăs'ouq yaun-ne-deh	အဆုတ်ရောင်နေတယ်
have a sore throat	leh-jaùn na-deh	လည်ချောင်းနာတယ်
have a stomachache	baiq na-deh	ဗိုက်နာတယ်
have sunstroke	ăpu-shaq-teh	အပူလျှပ်တယ်
have a toothache	thwà kaiq-teh	သွားကိုက်တယ်

HEALTH

WOMEN'S HEALTH

အမျိုးသမီးကျန်းမာရေး

Could I see a female doctor?
  ămyò-thămì-s'áya-wun-néh
  pyá-ló yá-mălà?

အမျိုးသမီးဆရာဝန်နဲ့
ပြလို့ရမလား။

I'm pregnant.
  cămá ko-wun shí-deh

ကျွန်မ ကိုယ်ဝန်ရှိတယ်။

I think I'm pregnant.
  ko-wun shí-deh t'in-deh

ကိုယ်ဝန်ရှိတယ် ထင်တယ်။

I'm on the Pill.
  cămá tà-zè sà-ne-deh

ကျွန်မတားဆေး စားနေတယ်။

I haven't had my period for ...
weeks.
  cămá ya-thi măla-da
  ... paq shí-bi

ကျွန်မ ရာသီမလာတာ ...
ပတ်ရှိပြီ။

I'd like to use contraception.
  cămá pătí-than-de tà-jin-deh

ကျွန်မ ပဋိသန္ဓေ တားချင်တယ်။

I'd like to have a pregnancy test.
  cămá ko-wun siq-c'in-deh

ကျွန်မ ကိုယ်ဝန် စစ်ချင်တယ်။

abortion	ko-wun p'yeq-c'á-jìn	ကိုယ်ဝန်ဖျက်ချခြင်း
cystitis	s'ì-ein-yaun-jìn	ဆီးအိမ်ယောင်ခြင်း
contraceptives	pătí-than-de tà-zè	ပဋိသန္ဓေ တားဆေး
menstruation	ya-thi la-deh	ရာသီလာတယ်။
miscarriage	ko-wun pyeq-cá-jìn	ကိုယ်ဝန်ပျက်ကျခြင်း
period pain	ya-thi-la-da kaiq-c'in	ရာသီလာတာကိုက်ခြင်း
the Pill	tà-zè	တားဆေး
thrush	meìn-má ko-ìn-ga	မိန်းမကိုယ်အင်္ဂါ
	yà-yan-jìn	ယားယံခြင်း

PARTS OF THE BODY

My ... hurts.

cănáw/cămá ... na-deh (m/f)

ခန္ဓာကိုယ်အစိတ်အပိုင်းများ

ကျွန်တော်/ကျွန်မ ... နာတယ်။

arm	leq-maùn	လက်မောင်း
back	càw-goùn	ကျောကုန်း
blood	thwè	သွေး
chest	yin-baq	ရင်ဘတ်
ear	năyweq	နားရွက်
eye	myeq-sí	မျက်စိ
hand	leq	လက်
head	gaùn	ခေါင်း
heart	hnăloùn	နှလုံး
kidney	cauq-kaq	ကျောက်ကပ်

leg/foot	c'e-dauq	ခြေထောက်
liver	ăthèh	အသည်း
lungs	ăs'ouq	အဆုတ်
muscle	cweq-thà	ကြွက်သား
nose	hnăk'aùn	နှာခေါင်း
shoulder	păk'oùn	ပခုံး
stomach	ăsa-ein/baiq	အစာအိမ်/ဗိုက်
skin	ăye-byà	အရေပြား
throat	leh-jaùn	လည်ချောင်း
tooth	thwà	သွား
upper arm	leq-maùn	လက်မောင်း

HEALTH

AT THE CHEMIST
ဆေးဆိုင်မှာ

See also page 107 in the Shopping chapter.

I need something for ...
  s'è-lo-aq-teh
  ... ဆေးလိုအပ်တယ်။

Do I need a prescription?
  s'è-nyùn pyá-yá-mălà?
  ဆေးညွှန်းပြရမလား။

I have a prescription.
  cănaw-hma s'è-nyùn shí-deh (m)
  ကျွန်တော်မှာ ဆေးညွှန်ရှိတယ်။

How many tablets a day?
  tăné-ko beh-hnălòun-lèh?
  တစ်နေ့ ကို ဘယ်နှလုံးလဲ။

What medicine is this?
  di-s'è ba-s'è-lèh?
  ဒီဆေး ဘာဆေးလဲ။

dosage directions	s'è ăhnyùn	ဆေးအညွှန်း
prescription	s'è-za	ဆေးစာ

Do you have ... ?   ... shí-là?   ... ရှိလား။
Where can I   ... beh-hma   ... ဘယ်မှာဝယ်ရမလဲ။
buy ... ?   weh-yá-mălèh?

antibiotics	an-ti-bà-yàw-tiq	အန်တီဘားရောတစ်
antiseptic	lèin-zè	လိမ်းဆေး
aspirin	eq-săpărin	အက်စပရင်
bandage	paq-tì	ပတ်တီး
Band-aids	păla-săta	ပလာစတာ
condoms	kun-dum	ကွန်ဒမ်
cotton wool	gùn	ဂွမ်း
cough medicine	c'àun-zò-pyauq-s'è	ချောင်းဆိုးပျောက်ဆေး
eye drops	myeq-sìn-ye	မျက်စဉ်းရည်
plaster	pălasăta	ပလာစတာ
sleeping pill	eiq-s'è	အိပ်ဆေး
syringe	s'è-dò-aq	ဆေးထိုးအပ်
thermometer	bădà-dain	ပြဒါးတိုင်

HEALTH

AT THE DENTIST

သွားဘက်ဆရာဝန်ဆီမှာ

Are you a dentist?
    hkămyà/shin
    thwà-s'ăya-wun-là? (m/f)

ခင်ဗျား/ရှင် သွားဆရာဝန်လား။။

My tooth hurts.
    cănáw/cămá
    thwà kaiq-teh (m/f)

ကျွန်တော်/ကျွန်မ
သွားကိုက်တယ်။။

This tooth is broken.
    di-thwà cò-thwà-bi

ဒီသွားကျိုးသွားပြီ။။

This tooth is chipped.
    di-thwà péh-ne-deh

ဒီသွားပဲ့နေတယ်။။

I've lost a filling.
    thwà-ba-dà
    pyouq-t'weq-thwà-bi

သွားဖာထားတာ
ပြုတ်ထွက်သွားပြီ။။

Will you have take the tooth out?
    thwà hnouq-săya lo-dhălà?

သွားနှုတ်စရာ လိုသလား။။

Please don't take it out.
    măhnouq-pa-néh

မနှုတ်ပါနဲ့။။

Can the tooth be repaired?
    thwà pyin-ló yá-là?

သွားပြင်လို့ ရလား။။

Can you fill the cavity?
    thwà p'a-nain-dhălà?

သွားဖာနိုင်သလား။။

Please give me an anaesthetic.
    toun-zè t'ò-pè-ba

ထုံဆေးထိုးပေးပါ။။

TIME, DATES & FESTIVALS

The Buddhist lunar calendar is used for religious holidays, so these fall on different dates every year. Most other national holidays follow the Western calendar. The seven-day week, with Saturday and Sunday as non-working days, is used and time is reckoned by the Western 12-hour system.

TELLING THE TIME

အချိန်ပြောခြင်း

What time is it?
  beh-ăc'ein-shí-bi-lèh?　　　　ဘယ်အချိန်ရှိပြီလဲ။

When? (in the past)
  beh-doùn-gá-lèh?　　　　ဘယ်တုန်းကလဲ။

When? (in the future)
  beh-dáw-lèh?　　　　ဘယ်တော့လဲ။

At what time?
  beh-ăc'ein-hma-lèh?　　　　ဘယ်အချိန်မှာလဲ။

7 am
  măneq k'ú-hnăna-yi　　　　မနက် ခုနစ်နာရီ

12 noon
  né-leh s'éh-hnăna-yi/mún-déh　　　　နေ့လယ်ဆယ့်နှစ်နာရီ/မွန်းတည့်

1 pm
  né-leh tăna-yi　　　　နေ့လယ် တစ်နာရီ

4.30 pm
  nyá-ne lè-na-yi-gwèh　　　　ညနေ လေးနာရီခွဲ

9 pm
  nyá kò-na-yi　　　　ညကိုးနာရီ

10.15 pm
  nyá s'eh-na-yi s'éh-ngà-măniq　　　　ည ဆယ်နာရီဆယ့်ငါးမိနစ်

12 midnight
  nyá s'éh-hnăna-yi　　　　ညဆယ့်နှစ်နာရီ

3.25 am
  măneq thoùn-na-yi
  hnăs'éh-ngà-măniq　　　　မနက်သုံးနာရီနှစ်ဆယ့်ငါးမိနစ်

MONTHS

လနာမည်များ

The lunar calendar does not correspond to the Western calendar – the following are the approximate equivalents:

	SOLAR	LUNAR
January (Pyatho)	zan-năwa-ri ဇန်နဝါရီ	pya-dho ပြာသို
February (Tabodwe)	p'e-băwa-ri ဖေဖော်ဝါရီ	tăbó-dwéh တပို့တွဲ
March (Tabaung)	maq မတ်	tăbaùn တပေါင်း
April (Tagu)	e-pyi ဧပြီ	tăgù တန်ခူး
May (Kason)	me မေ	kăs'oun ကဆုန်
June (Nayon)	zun ဇွန်	năyoun နယုန်
July (Waso)	zu-lain ဇူလိုင်	wa-zo ဝါဆို
August (Wagaung)	àw-gouq သြဂုတ်	wa-gaun ဝါခေါင်
September (Tawthalin)	seq-tin-ba စက်တင်ဘာ	taw-dhălìn တော်သလင်း
October (Thadingyut)	auq-to-ba အောက်တိုဘာ	thădìn-juq သီတင်းကျွတ်
November (Tazaungmon)	no-win-ba နိုဝင်ဘာ	tăzaun-moùn တန်ဆောင်မုန်း
December (Nattaw)	di-zin-ba ဒီဇင်ဘာ	nădaw နတ်တော်

The lunar year starts after the Thingyan water festival with Tagu, generally in mid-April. To bring the lunar year back into step with the seasons, a second month of Waso is added approximately every four years (a wa-t'aq or leap year). In these years (eg, 2001), there is a First Waso (păt'ămá wa-zo, ပထမဝါဆို) and a Second Waso (dú-tí-yá wa-zo, ဒုတိယဝါဆို). Each lunar month begins with the day after the new moon, has 14 days of waxing moon, the full moon day (which is often a religious festival), then 13 or 14 days of waning moon and the last day of the new moon.

waxing moon	lá-zàn	လဆန်း
full moon day	lá-byé-né	လပြည့်နေ့
waning moon	lá-zouq	လဆုတ်
new moon day (no moon visible)	lá-gweh-né	လကွယ်နေ့

year	hniq	နှစ်
month	lá	လ
week	dăpaq	တစ်ပတ်
day (24 hours)	yeq	ရက်
day (daytime)	né	နေ့
night	nyá	ည
hour	na-yi	နာရီ
minute	măniq	မိနစ်

DAYS OF THE WEEK

နေ့နာမည်များ

Sunday	tănìn-gănwe-né	တနင်္ဂနွေနေ့
Monday	tănìn-la-né	တနင်္လာနေ့
Tuesday	in-ga-né	အင်္ဂါနေ့
Wednesday	bouq-dăhù-né	ဗုဒ္ဓဟူးနေ့
Thursday	ca-dhăbădè-né	ကြာသပတေးနေ့
Friday	thauq-ca-né	သောကြာနေ့
Saturday	săne-né	စနေနေ့

DATES　　　　　　　　　　　　　　　ရက်စွဲများ

The Burmese calendar, still used for some purposes, started with the lunar year corresponding to 638/639 AD. This is known as the Sakkaraj or Thagayit (dhăgăyiq, သက္ကရာဇ်) era. For most purposes, however, the Christian era (Gregorian calendar) is now used instead.

To give a date in Burmese, you start with the year, then the month, the day (or phase of moon day for the lunar calendar), and then sometimes the day of the week. Note the slightly different form (with byé, ပြည့်, instead of k'ú, ခု) when the year ends in a zero.

(Friday) 10 August 2001

　hnă-t'aún-tă-k'ú-hniq àw-gouq-lá
　s'eh-yeq-né (thauq-ca-né)
　၂၀၀၁ခုနှစ်　သြဂုတ်လ(၁၀)ရက်နေ့　(သောကြာနေ့)

23 December 1997

　(tă)t'aún-kò-ya-kò-zéh-k'ú-hnăk'ú-hniq
　di-zin-ba-lá hnăs'eh-thoùn-yeq-né
　၁၉၉၇ခုနှစ် ဒီဇင်ဘာလာ(၂၃)ရက်နေ့

March 1990

　(tă)t'aún-kò-ya-kò-zeh-byé-hniq maq-lá
　၁၉၉၀ပြည့်နှစ် မတ်လ

10th waning day of Pyatho 1358 (= 1995)

　(dhăgăyiq) t'aún-thoùn-ya-ngà-zéh-shiq-k'ú-hniq
　pya-dho lá-zouq s'eh-yeq-né
　သက္ကရာဇ်၁၃၅၈ခုနှစ်ပြာသိုလဆုတ်(၁၀)ရက်နေ့

WATCH, BELL!

In some towns you may still hear the traditional
three-hour watch bells, especially at night.

PRESENT

ပစ္စုပ္ပန်

this morning	di măneq	ဒီမနက်
this afternoon	di né-gìn	ဒီနေ့ခင်း
tonight	di nyá	ဒီည
this week	di paq	ဒီပတ်
this month	di lá	ဒီလ
now	ăkú	အခု
right now	ăkú c'eq-c'ìn	အခုချက်ချင်း

PAST

အတိတ်

yesterday morning	măné-măneq-ká	မနေ့မနက်က
yesterday night	măné-nyá-gá	မနေ့ညက
last month	pì-géh-téh lá	ပြီးခဲ့တဲ့လ
(half an hour) ago	lun-kéh-déh (na-yi-weq)-ká	လွန်ခဲ့တဲ့ (နာရီဝက်)က
(three) days ago	lun-kéh-déh (thoùn)yeq-ká	လွန်ခဲ့တဲ့ (သုံး)ရက်က
since (May)	(me)-lá-gá-dèh-gá	(မေ)လကတည်းက

FUTURE

အနာဂတ်

tomorrow afternoon	măneq-p'yan né-gìn	မနက်ဖြန်နေ့ခင်း
tomorrow evening	măneq-p'yan nyá-ne	မနက်ဖြန်ညနေ
next month	nauq-lá	နောက်လ
next year	nauq-hniq	နောက်နှစ်
in (five) minutes	nauq-(ngà)-măniq	နောက် (ငါး)မိနစ်
in (six) days	nauq-(c'auq)-yeq	နောက် (ခြောက်)ရက်
within an hour/month	tăna-yi/tălá ădwìn	တစ်နာရီ/တစ်လ အတွင်း
until (June)	(zun)-lá ăt'í	(ဇွန်လ)အထိ

DURING THE DAY တစ်နေ့တာ

The day is divided into four parts:

morning (6 am to midday)	**măneq**	မနက်
early afternoon (midday to 3 pm)	**né-leh**	နေ့လယ်
afternoon/evening (3 to 7 pm)	**nyá-ne**	ညနေ
night (7 pm to 6 am)	**nyá**	ည

There are also special words for midday and midnight:

midday	**mùn-déh**	မွန်းတည့်
midnight	**thăgaun**	သန်းခေါင်

USEFUL PHRASES အသုံးဝင်သောဝေါဟာရများ

What time is it?
beh-ăc'ein shí-bi-lèh? ဘယ်အချိန်ရှိပြီလဲ။

How long will it take?
beh-lauq ca-ja thwà-yá-mălèh? ဘယ်လောက် ကြာကြာသွားရမလဲ။

When will it get dark?
beh-dáw mò-c'ouq-mălèh? ဘယ်တော့မိုးချုပ်မလဲ။

It is late. (of time)
nauq-cá-deh နောက်ကျတယ်။

What day (of the week) is it?
di-né ba-né-lèh? ဒီနေ့ဘာနေ့လဲ။

What is the date?
di-né beh-hnăyeq-né-lèh? ဒီနေ့ဘယ်နှစ်ရက်နေ့လဲ။

HOLIDAYS   ရုံးပိတ်ရက်နှင့်ပွဲတော်များ

Holidays based on the Western calendar are:

Independence Day
    luq-laq-yè-né   လွတ်လပ်ရေးနေ့
    (4 January, commemorating independence in 1948)

Union Day
    pye-daun-zú-né   ပြည်ထောင်စုနေ့
    (12 February, commemorating the signing of the Panglong
    Agreement in 1947)

Peasants Day
    taun-thu-leh-dhămà-né   တောင်သူလယ်သမားနေ့
    (2 March)

Armed Forces Day
    taq-mădaw-né   တပ်မတော်နေ့
    (27 March, commemorates the founding of the Burma Inde-
    pendence Army)

Workers Day
    ălouq-thămà-né   အလုပ်သမားနေ့
    (1 May)

Martyrs Day
    a-za-ni-né   အာဇာနည်နေ့
    (19 July, commemorating the 1947 assassination of Gen-
    eral Aung San and six other leaders)

Christmas Day
    k'ăriq-sămaq-pwèh-daw-né   ခရစ္စမတ်ပွဲတော်နေ့
    (25 December)

Lunar calendar holidays are:

Karen New Year
    kăyin-hniq-thiq-kù-né   ကရင်နှစ်သစ်ကူးနေ့
    (first waxing day of Pyatho)

Tabaung Festival
    tăbaun-pwèh-daw   တပေါင်းပွဲတော်
    (full moon of Tabaung)

TIME, DATES & FESTIVALS

Thingyan Water Festival
thăjan-pwèh-daw   သင်္ကြန်ပွဲတော်
(four days in mid April)

Buddha's Birthday
nyaun-ye-thùn-pwèh-daw   ညောင်ရေသွန်း ပွဲတော်
(full moon of Kason)

Buddhist Lent begins
dămăseq-ca-né   ဓမ္မစကြာနေ့
(full moon of Waso)

End of Lent
ăbí-dăma-né   အဘိဓမ္မာနေ့
(full moon of Thadingyut)

Festival of Lights
tăzaun-dain-pwèh-daw   တန်ဆောင်တိုင်ပွဲတော်
(full moon of Tazaungmon)

National Day
ămyò-dhà-né   အမျိုးသားနေ့
(10th waning day of Tazaungmon, commemorates the 1920
student boycott)

There are also religious festivals on other full moon days and
Buddhist observances and special events also take place on the
eighth waxing, eighth waning and new moon days of each lunar
month, particularly in Mandalay. These four days are known as
ú-bouq-né (ဥပုသ်နေ့). The three months of Lent, at the peak of
the rainy season, are the usual time for men and boys to enter
the monastery. Marriages are put on hold and monks are not
allowed to travel.

TIME TIPS

'When?' is beh-doùn-gá-lèh? in the past, and beh-dáw-lèh?
in the future. 'What time is it?' is beh-ăc'ein shí-bi-lèh?

Many festivals or 'pwes' in Myanmar are religious, but not all are Buddhist. For example, the spirits (naq, နတ်) are honoured at Taungbyone (taun-byoùn, တောင်ပြွန်), 30km north of Mandalay, in the week before the full moon of Wagaung. Individuals may also put on a festival and some temple festivals may include drama, comedy, puppets or dancing. Generally, pwes are held at night.

dance/comedy	ănyeín-pwèh	အငြိမ့်ပွဲ
dancing/singing chorus	yeìn	ယိမ်း
dramatic performance	zaq-pwèh	ဇာတ်ပွဲ
puppet show	youq-thè-pwèh	ရုပ်သေးပွဲ
temple festival	pwèh-daw	ပွဲတော်
spirit festival	naq-pwèh	နတ်ပွဲ

BIRTHDAYS
မွေးနေ့

When's your birthday?
mwè-né beh-dáw-lèh? မွေးနေ့ ဘယ်တော့လဲ။

My birthday is on (25 January).
cănáw mwè-né-gá ကျွန်တော်မွေးနေ့က
(25 zan-năwa-ri) (m) (၂၅ ဇန်နဝါရီ)။

Happy birthday!
mwè-né min-gălá! မွေးနေ့ မင်္ဂလာ။

WEDDINGS
လက်ထပ် မင်္ဂလာပွဲ

Congratulations!	goun-yu-ba-deh!	ဂုဏ်ယူပါတယ်။
engagement	sé-saq-pwèh	စေ့စပ်ပွဲ
honeymoon	pyà-ye-sàn-k'àyì	ပျားရည်စမ်းခရီး
wedding	leq-t'aq-pwèh	လက်ထပ်ပွဲ
wedding anniversary	min-gălá hniq-paq-leh	မင်္ဂလာနှစ်ပတ်လည်

TOASTS & CONDOLENCES

ဆုတောင်းဂုဏ်ပြုခြင်းနှင့်
ဝမ်းနည်းကြောင်းပြောခြင်း

Bon appetit!	thoùn-zaun-ba!	သုံ:ဆောင်ပါ။
Cheers!	c'ì-yà!	ချီ:ယာ:။
Bon voyage!	c'àw-jàw màw-màw yauq-ba-se!	ချောချောမောမော ရောက်ပါစေ။

Sickness

နေမကောင်းဖြစ်ခြင်း

Get well soon!
    myan-myan theq-tha-ba-se!   မြန်မြန်သက်သာပါစေ။

Death

သေဆုံးခြင်း

I'm very sorry.
    seiq măkaùn-săya-bèh   စိတ်မကောင်းစရာပဲ။

My deepest sympathy.
    ăyàn-wùn-nèh-ba-deh   အရမ်:ဝမ်:နည်:ပါတယ်။

My thoughts are with you.
    cănaw ko-jìn-sà-deh (m)   ကျွန်တော်ကိုယ်ချင်းစာတယ်။

Luck

ကံကောင်းခြင်း

Good luck!	kan-kaùn-ba-ze!	ကံကောင်းပါစေ။
Hope it goes well!	ăs'in-pye-ba-ze!	အဆင်ပြေပါစေ။
What bad luck!	kan s'ò-laiq-ta!	ကံဆို:လိုက်တာ။
Never mind!	keiq-sá măshí-ba-bù!	ကိစ္စမရှိပါဘူး။

TIME, DATES & FESTIVALS

CARDINAL NUMBERS

ဂဏန်း

1	၁	tiq/tă	တစ်/တ
2	၂	hniq/hnă	နှစ်/နှ
3	၃	thoùn	သုံး
4	၄	lè	လေး
5	၅	ngà	ငါး
6	၆	c'auq	ခြောက်
7	၇	k'un-hniq/k'un-hnă	ခုနစ်/ခုနှ
8	၈	shiq	ရှစ်
9	၉	kò	ကိုး
10	၁၀	(tă)s'eh	(တစ်)ဆယ်
11	၁၁	s'éh-tiq	ဆယ့်တစ်
12	၁၂	s'éh-hniq	ဆယ့်နှစ်
20	၂၀	hnăs'eh	နှစ်ဆယ်
35	၃၅	thoùn-zéh-ngà	သုံးဆယ့်ငါး
100	၁၀၀	tăya	တစ်ရာ
1,000	၁၀၀၀	(tă)t'aun	(တစ်)ထောင်
10,000	၁၀၀၀၀	(tă)thaùn	(တစ်)သောင်း
100,000	၁၀၀၀၀၀	(tă)theìn	(တစ်)သိန်း
million	၁၀၀၀၀၀၀	(tă)thàn	(တစ်)သန်း

One hundred thousand is often called one lakh.

HOW MUCH?

'How much?' is beh-lauq-lèh?, 'How much is the room?' is ăk'àn-k'á beh-lauq-lèh?, and 'How many?' is beh-hnă + counter + lèh?.

NUMBERS & AMOUNTS

To put a number together, start from the highest number and work down:

144,285 (people)
tătheìn-lè-thaùn-lè-daun-hnăyá-shiq-s'éh-ngà (yauq)
တစ်သိန်းလေးသောင်းလေးထောင်နှစ်ရာ့ရှစ်ဆယ့်ငါးယောက်

21 (round things)
hnăs'éh-tă-(loùn)   နှစ်ဆယ့်တစ်(လုံး)

15 books
sa-ouq s'éh-ngà-ouq   စာအုပ်ဆယ့်ငါးအုပ်

ORDINAL NUMBERS   အစဉ်ပြကိန်း

first	păt'ămá	ပထမ
second	dú-tí-yá	ဒုတိယ
third	tá-tí-yá	တတိယ
fourth	zătouq-t'á	စတုတ္ထ

COUNTERS   အရေအတွက်ပစ္စည်း

Whenever you count things in
Burmese, you must put in a
counter (also known as a classifier) after the number. These
always come after the noun
counted. It's something like
saying 'three items of clothing'
or 'three slices of cheese'.

Buddha, temples	s'u	ဆု
monks, royalty	pà/bà	ပါး
other high-status humans, and a formal, written form of yauq	ù	ဦး
people	yauq	ယောက်
animals	kaun/gaun	ကောင်
plants, rope, thread, hair	pin/bin	ပင်
round things, fruit, houses, furniture, machines	loùn	လုံး
flat things	c'aq/jaq	ချပ်
long things, teeth, fingers, toes, needles, legs, knives, pencils	c'aùn/jaùn	ချောင်း
clothing	t'eh/deh (lit: cloth)	ထည်
written things, tickets, letters, newspapers	saun/zaun	စောင်
tools, instruments	leq (lit: hand)	လက်
vehicles (large/small)	sìn/sì	စင်း/စီး
books	ouq	အုပ်
rings, other ring-shaped things	kwìn/gwìn	ကွင်း
leaves (including paper)	yweq	ရွက်

If you are giving a measure (miles, cups etc) after the noun, then you don't need another counter (see Shopping, page 109); groups and round numbers work the same. And if all this seems too complicated, just use the universal counter k'ú (ခု) which can be used with any inanimate noun; but not with monks, people or animals.

MONEY

ငွေကြေး

The currency is the caq (ကျပ်), which is divided into 100 pyà (ပြား). As in most languages, there are special words for some coins as well, but coins have now disappeared from circulation. Note that for round amounts of money (10, 100, 1,000 and so on) you should use ngwe, literally 'silver', before the round number, rather than caq after it.

1 kyat note	tăjaq-tan	တစ်ကျပ်တန်
5 kyat note	ngà-jaq-dan	ငါးကျပ်တန်
10 kyat note	ngwe tăs'eh-dan	ငွေတစ်ဆယ်တန်
15 kyat note	s'éh-ngà-jaq-tan	ဆယ့်ငါးကျပ်တန်
20 kyat note	hnăs'eh-jaq-tan	နှစ်ဆယ်ကျပ်တန်
45 kyat note	lè-zéh-ngà-jaq-tan	လေးဆယ့်ငါးကျပ်တန်
50 kyat note	ngà-zéh-jaq-tan	ငါးဆယ့်ကျပ်တန်
90 kyat note	kò-zéh-tan	ကိုးဆယ်တန်
100 kyat note	tăya-tan	တစ်ရာတန်
200 kyat note	hnăya-tan	နှစ်ရာတန်
500 kyat note	ngà-ya-tan	ငါးရာတန်
1000 kyat	ngwe tăt'aun	ငွေတစ်ထောင်

Foreign exchange certificates (FECs) were introduced in 1993. While officially called nain-ngan-jà-ngwe-lèh-leq-hmaq (နိုင်ငံခြားငွေလဲလှက်မှတ်), they are more commonly known as FEC (အက်ဖ်အီးစီး) or 'Burma dollar' (ဗမာ ဒေါ်လာ).

FRACTIONS అపిုင်းကိန်း

half	tăweq	တစ်ဝက်
a third	thoùn-boún-tăboun	သုံးပုံတစ်ပုံ
a quarter	lè-boún-tăboun/dăzeiq	လေးပုံတစ်ပုံ/တစ်စိတ်
five-eighths	shiq-poún ngà-boun	ရှစ်ပုံ၌ါးပုံ

NUMBERS & AMOUNTS

USEFUL AMOUNTS အသုံးဝင်သောပမာဏ

How much?	beh-lauq-lèh?	ဘယ်လောက်လဲ။
How many?	beh-hnăkú-lèh?	ဘယ်နှစ်ခုလဲ။
Could you	cănaw-go	ကျွန်တော်ကို ...
please give me ...	... pè-nain-mălà? (m)	ပေးနိုင်မလား။
I need ...	... lo-aq-teh	... လိုအပ်တယ်။
count	ye-deh	ရေတယ်
double	hnăs'á	နှစ်ဆ
dozen	da-zin	ဒါဇင်
enough	loun-loun-lauq-lauq	လုံလုံလောက်လောက်

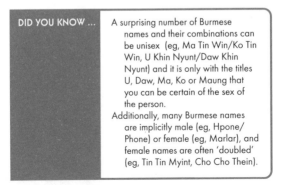

DID YOU KNOW ... A surprising number of Burmese names and their combinations can be unisex (eg, Ma Tin Win/Ko Tin Win, U Khin Nyunt/Daw Khin Nyunt) and it is only with the titles U, Daw, Ma, Ko or Maung that you can be certain of the sex of the person.

Additionally, many Burmese names are implicitly male (eg, Hpone/ Phone) or female (eg, Marlar), and female names are often 'doubled' (eg, Tin Tin Myint, Cho Cho Thein).

NUMBERS & AMOUNTS

a few	nèh-nèh	နည်းနည်း
(just) a little	nèh-nèh-lè-bèh	နည်းနည်းလေးပဲ
less	po-bì-nèh-nèh	ပိုပြီးနည်းနည်း
a lot	myà-myà	များများ
more	po-bì-myà-myà	ပိုပြီးများများ
once	tăk'auq-tèh	တစ်ခေါက်တည်
pair	yan/soun/zoun	ရန်/စုံ
some	tăc'ó	တချို့
too many/much	ăyàn myà-deh	အရမ်းများတယ်
twice	hnăcein	နှစ်ကြိမ်
zero	thoun-nyá	သုည

EMERGENCIES

Help!	keh-ba!	ကယ်ပါ။
Watch out!	dhădí t'à-ba!	သတိထား ပါ။
Go away!	thwà-zàn!	သွား စမ်း။
Stop!	yaq!	ရပ်။
Don't do it!	mălouq-néh!	မလုပ်နဲ့။
Thief!	thăk'ò!	သူခိုး။
Pickpocket!	găbaiq-hnaiq!	ခါ ပိုက်နှိုက်။

It's an emergency.
ăyè-p'yiq-ne-bi
အရေး ဖြစ်နေပြီ။

Could you help us please?
cănaw-dó-go
ku-nyi-nain-mălà? (m)
ကျွန်တော်တို့ကို
ကူညီနိုင်မလာ ။

I am lost.
làn pyauq-thwà-bi
လမ်း ပျောက်သွား ပြီ။

Where are the toilets?
ein-tha beh-hma-lèh?
အိမ်သာဘယ်မှာလဲ။

Call the police!
yèh kaw-pè-ba!
ရဲခေါ် ပေ ပါ။

Where's the police station?
yèh săk'àn beh-nà-mălèh?
ရဲစခန်းဘယ်နားမှာလဲ။

We want to report an offence.
cănaw-dó
ăhmú-p'wín-jin-deh (m)
ကျွန်တော်တို့
အမှုဖွင့်ချင်တယ်။

I've been raped.
mú-dèin cín-k'an-yá-deh
မုဒိမ်းကျင့်ခံရတာယ်။

I've been robbed.
ăk'ò-k'an-yá-deh
အခိုး ခံရတယ်။

My pocket was picked.
găbaiq-hnaiq k'an-yá-deh
ခါ ပိုက်နှိုက်ခံရတယ်။

My camera was stolen.
cănáw/cămá kin-măra
k'ò-k'an-yá-deh (m/f)
ကျွန်တော်/ ကျွန်မ
ကင်မရာခိုး ခံရတယ်။

EMERGENCIES

I've lost my ...	cănaw/cămá ...	ကျွန်တော်/ကျွန်မ ...
	pyauq-thwà-deh (m/f)	ပျောက်သွားတယ်။
bag	eiq	အိတ်
customs form	kaq-sătan-poun-zan	ကပ်စတန်ပုံစံ
money	paiq-s'an	ပိုက်ဆံ
passport	paq-săpó	ပတ်စပို့
travellers cheques	k'ăyì c'eq-leq-hmaq	ခရီးချက်လက်မှတ်
wallet	paiq-s'an-eiq	ပိုက်ဆံအိတ်

Could I use the telephone?
teh-li-p'oùn k'ăná
s'eq-ló-yá-là?
တယ်လီဖုန်း ခဏ
ဆက်လို့ရလား။

Call a doctor!
s'ăya-wun-go k'aw-pè-ba!
ဆရာဝန်ကို ခေါ်ပေးပါ။

Call an ambulance!
lu-na-din-yin k'aw-pè-ba!
လူနာတင်ယာဉ်ခေါ်ပေးပါ။

I am ill.
ne-măkàun-bù
နေမကောင်းဘူး။

I have (medical) insurance.
cănaw/cămá (s'è) a-má-gan
shí-ba-deh (m/f)
ကျွန်တော်/ကျွန်မ (ဆေး)
အာမခံ ရှိပါတယ်။

embassy	than-yoùn	သံရုံး
form	poun-zan	ပုံစံ
government official	wun-dàn	ဝန်တမ်း
immigration	lu-win-hmú	လူဝင်မှု
office	cì-jaq-yè-youn	ကြီးကြပ်ရေးရုံး
police	yèh/păleiq	ရဲ/ပုလိပ်

A

able, to be (can) (see also page 31)	... nain ...	... နိုင် ...
I can't do it.	mǎlouq-nain-bù.	မလုပ်နိုင်ဘူး။
about (approximately)	... lauq	... လောက်
above (on top of)	ǎpaw-hma	အပေါ်မှာ
abroad	nain-ngan-jà-hma	နိုင်ငံခြားမှာ
accept	leq-k'an-deh	လက်ခံတယ်
accidentally	mǎtaw-tǎs'á	မတော်တဆ
accommodation	ne-ya	နေရာ
addict (drug)	swèh-ne-déh-lu	စွဲနေတဲ့လူ
addiction (drug)	s'è-swèh-da	ဆေးစွဲတာ
address	leiq-sa	လိပ်စာ
administration	ouq-c'ouq-c'ìn	အုပ်ချုပ်ခြင်း
admission charge	win-cè	ဝင်ကြေး
admit (let in)	win-gwín pè-deh	ဝင်ခွင့်ပေးတယ်
advice	ǎcan	အကြံ
advise	ǎcan pè-deh	အကြံပေးတယ်
aeroplane	le-yin-byan	လေယာဉ်ပျံ
afraid, be	cauq-teh	ကြောက်တယ်
after (+ n)	... nauq	... နောက်
after (+ v)	... pì-dáw	... ပြီးတော့
again (+ v)	pyan ...	ပြန် ...
again (another time)	nauq-tǎk'a	နောက်တစ်ခါ
age	ǎtheq	အသက်
agree	thǎbàw-tu-deh	သဘောတူတယ်
agriculture	saiq-pyò-yè	စိုက်ပျိုးရေး
ahead	shé	ရှေ့
aid (n)	ǎku-ǎnyi	အကူအညီ
air-conditioned	èh-yà-kùn shí-deh	အဲယားကွန်း ရှိတယ်
air-conditioner	le-è-zeq	လေအေးစက်

airline	le-yin-byan koun-păni	လေယာဉ်ပျံကုမ္ပဏီ
airmail	le-jàun-za	လေကြောင်းစာ
airport	le-zeiq	လေဆိပ်
alarm clock	hnò-seq	နှိုးစက်
alcoholic	ăyeq-thămà	အရက်သမား
all	à-loùn	အားလုံး
allow	k'wín-pè-deh	ခွင့်ပေးတယ်
almost	lú-nì-nì	လုနီးနီး
alms bowl (of monk)	dhă-beiq	သပိတ်
alone (of person)	tăyauq-t'èh	တစ်ယောက်ထည်း
also	... lèh	... လည်း
always	ămyèh	အမြဲ
amazing	án-àw-săya	အံ့သြစရာ
	kaùn-deh	ကောင်းတယ်
ambassador	than-ămaq-cì	သံအမတ်ကြီး
ambulance	lu-na-din-yin	လူနာတင်ယာဉ်
among	ăleh-hma	အလယ်မှာ
ancient	shè-haùn-deh	ရှေးဟောင်းတယ်
and (n + n)	néh	နဲ့
and (v + v)	lèh	လည်
angry	seiq-s'ò-deh	စိတ်ဆိုးတယ်
animal	dăreiq-s'an	တိရစ္ဆာန်
answer (n)	ăp'ye	အဖြေ
answer (v)	p'ye-deh	ဖြေတယ်
ant	păyweq-s'eiq	ပရွက်ဆိတ်
antique	shè-haùn pyiq-sì	ရှေးဟောင်း ပစ္စည်း
appointment	c'eìn-t'à-da	ချိန်းထားတာ
approximately	... lauq	... လောက်
archaeology	shè-haùn thú-te-thá-ná	ရှေးဟောင်း သုတေသန
argue	săgà-myà-deh	စကားများတယ်
army (Myanmar)	taq-mădaw	တပ်မတော်

army (forces)	siq-taq	စစ်တပ်
arrest (v)	p'àn-deh	ဖမ်းတယ်
arrested	ăp'àn-k'an-yá-bi	အဖမ်းခံရပြီ
arrive	yauq-teh	ရောက်တယ်
art	ănú-pyin-nya	အနုပညာ
ashtray	s'è-leiq-pya-gweq	ဆေးလိပ်ပြာခွက်
ask	mè-deh	မေးတယ်
asleep	eiq-ne-deh	အိပ်နေတယ်
astrologer	be-din-s'ăya	ဗေဒင်ဆရာ
asylum (for refugee)	k'o-hloun-gwín	ခိုလှုံခွင့်
at	... hma	... မှာ
aunt	ădaw	အဒေါ်
automatically	ălo-lo	အလိုလို

B

baby	kălè	ကလေး
babysitter	kălè-deìn	ကလေးထိန်း
backpack	càw-pò-eiq	ကျောပိုးအိတ်
bad	s'ò-deh	ဆိုးတယ်
bag	eiq	အိတ်
baggage	thiq-ta/pyiq-sì	သေတ္တာ/ပစ္စည်း
ball	bàw-loùn	ဘောလုံး
bank	ban-daiq	ဘဏ်တိုက်
bar (place to drink)	ăyeq-s'ain	အရက်ဆိုင်
barbecue	ăsa-ăkin	အစာအကင်
barbershop	zăbin-hnyaq-s'ain	ဆံပင်ညှပ်ဆိုင်
basket	chìn-daùn	ခြင်းတောင်း
bat (animal)	lìn-nó	လင်းနို့
battery	beq-t'ări/daq-k'eh	ဘက်ထရီ/ဓါတ်ခဲ
be (see page 29)	–	–
be born	mwè-deh	မွေးတယ်
beach	pin-leh-gàn-je	ပင်လယ်ကမ်းခြေ
beard	mouq-s'eiq	မုတ်ဆိတ်

beautiful	hlá-deh	လှတယ်
because (+ n)	... mó-ló	... မို့လို့
because (+ v)	... ló	... လို့
bed	eiq-ya/gădin	အိပ်ရာ/ခုတင်
bedbug	jăbò	ကြမ်းပိုး
before (+ v)	mă ... k'in/gin	မ ... ခင်
beggar	dhădaùn-sà	သူတောင်းစား
behind	... nauq	... နောက်
bell	k'aùn-laùn	ခေါင်းလောင်း
below	... auq	... အောက်
beside	năbè-hma	နံဘေးမှာ
best	ăkaùn-zoùn	အကောင်းဆုံး
bet (v)	laùn-găsà-deh	လောင်းကစားတယ်
better	po-kaùn-deh	ပိုကောင်းတယ်
between	... cà	... ကြား
Bible	k'ăriq-yan-thăma-càn	ခရစ်ယာန် သမ္မာကျမ်း
bicycle	seq-beìn	စက်ဘီး
big	cì-deh	ကြီးတယ်
bill (account)	ngwe-daùn-hlwa	ငွေတောင်းလွှာ
bill (banknote)	ngwe-seq-ku	ငွေစက္ကူ
bird	hngeq	ငှက်
birthday	mwè-né	မွေးနေ့
bitter	k'à-deh	ခါးတယ်
bless	s'ú-pè-deh	ဆုပေးတယ်
blind	myeq-sí kàn-ne-deh	မျက်စိကန်းနေတယ်
boat (large)	thìn-bàw	သင်္ဘော
boat (small)	hle	လှေ
body	ko-k'an-da	ကိုယ်ခန္ဓာ
bone	ăyò	အရိုး
bomb	boùn	ဗုံး
Bon appetit!	thoùn-s'aun-ba!	သုံးဆောင်ပါ
book (n)	sa-ouq	စာအုပ်

bookshop	sa-ouq-s'ain	စာအုပ်ဆိုင်
I'm bored.	pyìn-deh	ပျင်းတယ်
boring	pyìn-săya kaùn-deh	ပျင်းစရာကောင်းတယ်
borrow	hngà-deh	ငှားတယ်
May I borrow this?	èh-da hngà-ló yá-là?	အဲ့ဒါငှားလို့ရလား။
boss (owner)	ălouq-shin	အလုပ်ရှင်
both (+ counter)	hnă ... săloùn	နှစ် ... စလုံး
bottle	pălìn	ပုလင်း
bottle opener	p'auq-dan	ဖောက်တံ
box (container)	thiq-ta/bù	သေတ္တာ/ဘူး
boxing	leq-hwé	လက်ဝှေ့
boy	kaun-lè	ကောင်လေး
boyfriend	yì-zà	ရည်းစား
bracelet	leq-kauq	လက်ကောက်
brave	yèh-deh	ရဲတယ်
break (rest) (n)	yaq-nà-jein	ရပ်နားချိန်
break (snap) (v)	cò-deh	ကျိုးတယ်
breakfast	măneq-sa	မနက်စာ
breathe	ătheq-shu-deh	အသက်ရှူတယ်
bribe (v)	laq-pè-deh	လာဘ်ပေးတယ်
bridge	dădà	တံတား
bright (shiny)	tauq-teh	တောက်တယ်
bright (clever)	t'eq-teh	ထက်တယ်
bring	yu-deh	ယူတယ်
Can you bring it?	èh-da yu-ló-yá-là?	အဲ့ဒါယူလို့ရလား။
We can bring one.	tăk'ú yu-nain-meh	တစ်ခုယူနိုင်မယ်။
broken	pyeq-thwà-bi	ပျက်သွားပြီ
broom	dăbyeq-sì	တံမြက်စည်း
bucket	ye-boùn	ရေပုံး
Buddha image	p'ăyà-s'in-dú-daw	ဘုရားဆင်းတုတော်
building	ăs'auq-ă-oun	အဆောက်အအုံ
bull	năthò	နွားသိုး

burn (v)	mì-tauq-laun-deh	မီးတောက်လောင်တယ်
bus	bas-kà	ဘတ်စ်ကား
bush	c'oun-bouq	ချုံပုတ်
business (company)	louq-ngàn	လုပ်ငန်း
business (trade)	sì-bwà-yè	စီးပွားရေး
busy	ălouq-myà-deh	အလုပ်များတယ်
but	da-be-méh	ဒါပေမဲ့
buy	weh-deh	ဝယ်တယ်

C

cafe	lăp'eq-ye-zain	လက်ဖက်ရည်ဆိုင်
camera	kin-măra	ကင်မရာ
camp (n)	săk'àn	စခန်း
camp (v)	săk'àn c'á-deh	စခန်းချတယ်
Can we camp here?	**di-hma săk'àn c'á-ló-yá-là?**	**ဒီမှာစခန်းချလို့ရလား။**
can (physically able) (v) (see also page 31)	... nain ...	... နိုင် ...
can (know) (v)	... taq/daq ...	... တတ် ...
Can you speak English?	**ìn-găleiq-zăgà pyàw-daq-thălà?**	**အင်္ဂလိပ်စကား ပြောတတ်သလား။**
can (v) (permissible)	yá-deh	ရတယ်
Can I take a photograph?	**daq-poun yaiq-ló yá-là?**	**ဓါတ်ပုံရိုက်လို့ရလား။**
You can't do it.	**măyá-bù**	**မရဘူး။**
can (tin)	than-bù	သံဘူး
can opener	p'auq-tan	ဖောက်တံ
candle	p'ăyaùn-dain	ဖယောင်းတိုင်
capital city	myó-daw	မြို့တော်
capitalism	ăyin-shin-săniq	အရင်းရှင်စနစ်
cards (playing)	p'èh	ဖဲ
care (about/for)	găyú saiq-teh	ဂရုစိုက်တယ်

careful (v)	dhǎdi t'à-deh	သတိထားတယ်
Be careful!	dhǎdi t'à-ba!	သတိထားပါ။
carry	theh-deh	သယ်တယ်
I'll carry it for you.	cǎnaw/cǎmá theh-pè-meh (m/f)	ကျွန်တော်/ကျွန်မ သယ်ပေးမယ်။
cashier	ngwe-gain	ငွေကိုင်
cave	gu	ဂူ
cemetery	thìn-gyàin	သချ္ုႋင်း
certain (sure)	the-ja-deh	သေချာတယ်
chance, by	mǎtaw-tǎs'á	မတော်တဆ
chair	kǎlǎt'ain	ကုလားထိုင်
change (money, clothes)	lèh-deh	လဲတယ်
change (trains, state)	pyaùn-deh	ပြောင်းတယ်
cheap	zè-pàw-deh	ဈေးပေါတယ်
cheat	lein-nya-deh	လိမ်ညာတယ်
chemist (pharmacy)	s'è-zain	ဆေးဆိုင်
Chiang Mai	zìn-meh	ဇင်းမယ်
child	kǎlè	ကလေး
choose	ywè-deh	ရွေးတယ်
Christmas	k'ǎriq-sǎmá pwèh-daw	ခရစ်စမတ်ပွဲတော်
cigarettes	si-gǎreq/s'è-leiq	စီးကရက်/ဆေးလိပ်
citizen	ǎmyò-dhà	အမျိုးသား
city	myó	မြို့
clean	thán-shìn-deh	သန့်ရှင်းတယ်
close (nearby)	di-nà-hma	ဒီနားမှာ
close (shut)	peiq-deh	ပိတ်တယ်
It's shut.	peiq-t'à-deh	ပိတ်ထားတယ်။
clothes	ǎwuq-ǎsà	အဝတ်အစား
cold (cool)	è-deh	အေးတယ်
colonel	bo-hmù-jì	ဗိုလ်မှူးကြီး

come	la-deh	လာတယ်
It's coming.	la-ne-bi	လာနေပြီ။
Can we come tomorrow?	măneq-p'yan la-yin yá-mălà?	မနက်ဖြန် လာရင် ရမလား။
comfortably	theq-taún-theq-tha	သက်သောင့်သက်သာ
commandeer	c'àw-s'wèh-deh	ချောဆွဲတယ်
communism	kun-myu-niq-săniq	ကွန်မြူနစ်စနစ်
company	koun-păni	ကုမ္ပဏီ
complex (adj)	shouq-teh	ရှုပ်တယ်
compound (garden)	wìn	ဝင်း
computer	kun-pyu-ta	ကွန်ပျူတာ
condom	kun-dun	ကွန်ဒွန်
constipated	wùn-c'ouq-teh	ဝမ်းချုပ်တယ်
contact lens	myeq-sí-kaq-myeq-hman	မျက်စိကပ်မျက်မှန်
contagious	kù-seq-taq-teh	ကူးစက်တတ်တယ်
contraceptive (pill)	tà-s'è	တားဆေး
convenient	ăs'in pye-deh	အဆင်ပြေတယ်
conversation	săgà-pyàw-da	စကားပြောတာ
cook (v)	c'eq-teh	ချက်တယ်
I enjoy cooking.	c'eq-ta-pyouq-ta wa-thá-na pa-deh	ချက်တာပြုပ်တာ ဝါသနာပါတယ်။
copy	kù-deh	ကူးတယ်
corner	t'aún/daún	ထောင့်
corrupt (adj)	laq-sà-deh	လာဘ်စားတယ်
corruption	laq-pè-laq-yu	လာဘ်ပေးလာဘ်ယူ
cost	cá-deh	ကျတယ်
How much does it cost?	beh-lauq-cá-lèh?	ဘယ်လောက်ကျလဲ။
count (v)	ye-deh	ရေတယ်
crazy	yù-deh	ရူးတယ်
credit card	ăcwè-weh kaq-pyà	အကြွေးဝယ်ကပ်ပြား
crop	kauq-pèh-thì-hnan	ကောက်ပဲသီးနှံ

cross (angry)	seiq-s'ò-deh	စိတ်ဆိုးတယ်
culture	yin-jè-hmú	ယဉ်ကျေးမှု
curtain	k'àn-zì/kălăga	ခန်းဆီး/ကန့်လန့်ကာ
customs	ăkauq-k'un	အကောက်ခွန်
cut (tree) (v)	k'ouq-teh	ခုတ်တယ်
cut (paper) (v)	p'yaq-teh	ဖြတ်တယ်

D

daily	né-dàin	နေ့တိုင်း
damp	so-t'àin-deh	စိုထိုင်းတယ်
dance	ká-deh	ကတယ်
dangerous	an-dăyeh shí-deh	အန္တရာယ်ရှိတယ်
dark (sky)	hmaun-deh	မှောင်တယ်
date (time)	yeq-swèh	ရက်စွဲ
daughter	thămì	သမီး
dawn	ăyoun	အရုဏ်
day	né	နေ့
dead	the-thwà-bi	သေသွားပြီ
deaf	nà pìn-deh	နားပင်းတယ်
decide	s'oùn-p'yaq-teh	ဆုံးဖြတ်တယ်
decision	s'oùn-p'yaq-c'eq	ဆုံးဖြတ်ချက်
delicious	ăyá-dha-shí-deh	အရသာရှိတယ်
democracy	di-mo-kăre-si	ဒီမိုကရေစီ
demonstration	s'an-dá-pyá-bwèh	ဆန္ဒပြပွဲ
depart (leave)	t'weq-deh	ထွက်တယ်
The plane departs at ...	le-yin-byan ... hma t'weq-ba-deh	လေယာဉ်ပျံ ... မှာ ထွက်ပါတယ်။
What time does it leave?	beh-ăc'ein t'weq-dhălèh?	ဘယ်အချိန် ထွက်သလဲ။
departure	t'weq-ta	ထွက်တာ
deposit (v)	aq-t'à-deh	အပ်ထားတယ်
destroy	p'yeq-s'ì-deh	ဖျက်ဆီးတယ

detain	t'ein-thein-deh	တိန်းသိန်းတယ်
development	tò-teq-hmú	တိုးတက်မှု
dictatorship	a-na-shin săniq	အာဏာရှင်စနစ်
dictionary	ăbí-dan	အဘိဓာန်
die	the-thwà-deh	သေသွားတယ်
different	kwèh-deh	ကွဲတယ်
It is different.	mătu-bù	မတူဘူး
difficult	k'eq-teh	ခက်တယ်
dinner (evening)	nyá-za	ညစာ
diplomat	than-tăman	သံတမန်
dirt	ănyiq-ăcè	အညစ်အကြေး
dirty	nyiq-paq-teh	ညစ်ပတ်တယ်
disadvantage	măkaùn-déh-ăc'eq	မကောင်းတဲ့အချက်
disagree	thăbàw mătu-bù	သဘောမတူဘူး
discount (v)	zè-sháw-deh	ဈေးလျှော့တယ်
discrimination	k'wèh-c'à-da	ခွဲခြားတာ
distant	wè-deh	ဝေးတယ်
divorce (v)	kwa-shìn-deh/ pyaq-sèh-deh	ကွာရှင်းတယ်/ ပြတ်စဲတယ်
do	louq-teh	လုပ်တယ်
I'll do it for you.	louq-pè-meh	လုပ်ပေးမယ်။
doctor	s'ăya-wun	ဆရာဝန်
doll	ăyouq	အရုပ်
donate	ăhlu kan-deh	အလှူခံတယ်
down	auq-ko	အောက်ကို
downstairs	auq-t'aq-hma	အောက်ထပ်မှာ
downtown	myó-leh-gaun	မြို့လယ်ခေါင်
dream (v)	eiq-meq-teh	အိပ်မက်တယ်
dried	c'auq	ခြောက်
drink (n)	thauq-săya	သောက်စရာ
drink (v)	thauq-teh	သောက်တယ်

drinkable water	thauq-ye	သောက်ရေ
drive (vehicle) (v)	maùn-deh	မောင်းတယ်
drought	mò k'aun-deh	မိုးခေါင်တယ်
drugs (medicine)	s'è-wà	ဆေးဝါး
drugs (narcotics)	mù-yiq-s'è-wà	မူးယစ်ဆေးဝါး
drum	boun	ဗုံ
drums (round rack)	s'àin-wàin	ဆိုင်းဝိုင်း
drunk (inebriated)	ăyeq-mù-deh	အရက်မူးတယ်
dry	c'auq	ခြောက်
dust	p'oun	ဖုံ
dustbin	ăhmaiq-poun	အမှိုက်ပုံ
duty (customs)	ăkauq-k'un	အကောက်ခွန်
duty (obligation)	wuq-tăyà	ဝတ္တရား
duty (on duty)	ta-wun shí-deh	တာဝန်ရှိတယ်။
dye (n)	s'ò-s'è	ဆိုးဆေး
dye (v)	s'ò-deh	ဆိုးတယ်

each (thing)	tăk'ú-zi	တစ်ခုစီ
each (person)	tăyauq-si	တစ်ယောက်စီ
early (adv)	sàw-zàw	စောစော
earnings, income	win-ngwe	ဝင်ငွေ
Earth (planet)	kăba-jo	ကမ္ဘာကြီဟ်
earth (soil)	mye-jì	မြေကြီး
earthquake	mye-ngălyin	မြေငလျင်
easy	lweh-deh	လွယ်တယ်
eat	sà-deh	စားတယ်
economy	si-bwà-yè	စီးပွားရေး
education	pyin-nya-yè	ပညာရေး
election	ywè-kauq-pwèh	ရွေးကောက်ပွဲ
electricity, electrical	hlyaq-siq	လျှပ်စစ်
elevator (lift)	daq-hle-gà	ဓါတ်လှေကား
embassy	than-yoùn	သံရုံး

employer	ălouq-shin	အလုပ်ရှင်
empty (finished)	koun-thwà-bi	ကုန်သွားပြီ
end (n)	ăs'òun	အဆုံး
'The End'	pì-bi	ပီးပြီ
energy	in-à	အင်အား
English	ìn-găleiq	အင်္ဂလိပ်
enjoy (oneself)	pyaw-shwin-deh	ပျော်ရွှင်တယ်
enjoy (doing)	wa-thá-na pa-deh	ဝါသနာပါတယ်
enough	lauq-teh	လောက်တယ်
enter	win-deh	ဝင်တယ်
entrance	win-bauq	ဝင်ပေါက်
envelope	sa-eiq	စာအိတ်
environment	paq-wùn-jin	ပတ်ဝန်းကျင်
equal	tu-nyi-deh	တူညီတယ်
especially	ăt'ù-dhăp'yín	အထူးသဖြင့်
ethical	cín-wuq-néh kaiq-nyi-deh	ကျင့်ဝတ်နဲ့ ကိုက်ညီတယ်
ethnic minority	tàin-yìn-dhà-lu-myò	တိုင်းရင်းသားလူမျိုး
evening	nyá-ne	ညနေ
event	p'yiq-yaq	ဖြစ်ရပ်
every	... tàin/dàin	... တိုင်း
every day	né-dàin	နေ့တိုင်း
everyone	lu-dàin	လူတိုင်း
everything	à-loùn	အားလုံး
exchange (v)	lèh-hleh-deh	လဲလှယ်တယ်
exhausted	pin-bàn-deh	ပင်ပန်းတယ်
exile (n)	pye-byè	ပြည်ပြေး
exit	t'weq-pauq	ထွက်ပေါက်
expensive	zè-cì-deh	ဈေးကြီးတယ်
experience	ătwé-ăcoun	အတွေ့အကြုံ
explain	shìn-pyá-deh	ရှင်းပြတယ်
export (v)	nain-ngan-gyà-ko	နိုင်ငံခြားကို
	tin-pó-deh	တင်ပို့တယ်
extra	ăpo	အပို

ENGLISH – BURMESE

F

face	myeq-hna	မျက်နှာ
false	mǎhman-bù	မမှန်ဘူး
family	mí-dhà-zú	မိသားစု
fan (hand-held)	yaq-taun	ယပ်တောင်
fan (ceiling)	pan-ka	ပန်ကာ
far	wè-deh	ဝေးတယ်
farm (not paddy) (n)	ya	ယာ
farm (paddy) (n)	leh	လယ်
farm (v)	leh-louq-deh/ ya-louq-deh	လယ်လုပ်တယ်/ ယာလုပ်တယ်
fast (not eat) (v)	ú-bouq saún-deh	ဥပုသ်စောင့်တယ်
fast (quick)	myan-deh	မြန်တယ်
fat	wá-deh	ဝတယ်
fault	ǎpyiq	အပြစ်
fee	ǎk'á-cè	အခကြေး
feel (touch) (v)	t'í-deh	ထိတယ်
feeling (sentiment)	k'an-zà-hmú	ခံစားမှု
ferry	gǎdó	ကူးတို့
festival	pwèh	ပွဲ
fever, to have a	p'yà-deh	ဖျားတယ်
few	nèh-deh	နည်းတယ်
fiancé(e)	sé-saq-t'à-déh-lu	စေ့စပ်ထားတဲ့လူ
film (movie)	youq-shin-kà	ရုပ်ရှင်ကား
film (roll of)	p'ǎlin	ဖလင်
fine (penalty)	dan-ngwe	ဒဏ်ငွေ
finger	leq-c'aùn	လက်ချောင်း
fingernail	leq-thèh	လက်သည်း
finish	pì-deh	ပြီးတယ်
fire	mì	မီး
firewood	t'ìn	ထင်း
flag	ǎlan	အလံ

DICTIONARY

F

flashlight (torch)	leq-hneiq-daq-mì	လက်နှိပ်ဓါတ်မီ
flat (apartment)	taiq-gàn	တိုက်ခန့်
flat (level)	pyin-deh	ပြင်တယ်
flavour	ăyădha	အရသာ
flea (louse)	ăhlè	အလေ့
flip-flops (thongs)	p'ănaq	ဖိနပ်
flood (v)	ye-ji-deh	ရေကြီ တယ်
floor (storey)	ăt'aq	အထပ်
floor	càn-byin	ကြမ် ပြင်
flour (wheat)	joun-moún	ဂျုံမုန့်
flower	pàn	ပန်
fluent	cwàn-jìn-deh	ကျွမ် ကျင် တယ်
fly (bird)	pyan-deh	ပျံတယ်
fly (go by plane)	le-yin-byan-néh thwà-deh	လေယာဉ်ပျံနဲ့ သွာ တယ်
fly (insect)	yin-kaun	ယင်ကောင်
follow	laiq-teh	လိုက်တယ်
food	ăsà-ăsa	အစာ အစာ
food poisoning	ăt'eq-lan-wùn-shàw	အထက်လန်ဝမ် လျှော
foot	c'e-dauq	ခြေထောက်
forced labour	louq-à-pè	လုပ်အာ ပေ
foreign	nain-ngan-jà	နိုင်ငံခြာ
foreigner	nain-ngan-jà-thà	နိုင်ငံခြာ သာ
forget	mé-deh	မေ့တယ်
I have forgotten.	mé-thwà-bi	မေ့သွာ ပြီ။
forgive	k'wín-hluq-teh	ခွင့်လွှတ်တယ်
fragile (things)	kwèh-lweh-deh	ကွဲလွယ်တယ်
free (of charge)	ălăgà/ăk'á-méh	အလကာ / အခမဲ့
free (not bound)	luq-laq-teh	လွတ်လပ်တယ်
free (release)	hluq-teh	လွှတ်တယ်
freeze	ye-k'èh-deh	ရေခဲတယ်
fresh (not stale)	laq-teh	လတ်တယ်
friend	thăngeh-jìn	သူငယ်ချင်
friendly	k'in-daq-teh	ခင်တတ်တယ်

ENGLISH – BURMESE

full	pyé-deh	ပြည့်တယ်
fun	ăpyaw-ăpà	အပျော်အပါ:
funny	yì-zăya kaùn-deh	ရယ်စရာ ကောင်းတယ်
fur	ămwè	အမွေး
future (n)	ăna-gaq	အနာဂတ်

G

game (match)	găzà-bwèh	ကစားပွဲ
garbage	ăhmaiq	အမှိုက်
garden	ú-yin	ဥယျာဉ်
gas	daq-ngwé	ဓါတ်ငွေ့
gas cylinder	daq-ngwé-ò	ဓါတ်ငွေ့အိုး
gate	dăgà-bauq	တံခါးပေါက်
generous	yeq-yàw-deh	ရက်ရောတယ်
genuine, real	siq-teh	စစ်တယ်
girl	meìn-kălè	မိန်းကလေး
girlfriend	yì-zà	ရည်းစား
give	pè-deh	ပေးတယ်

Give me ... | cănaw/cămá-go | ကျွန်တော်/ကျွန်မကို
... pè-ba (m/f) | ... ပေးပါ။

glass (of water)	p'an-gweq	ဖန်ခွက်
glasses	myeq-hman	မျက်မှန်
go	thwà-deh	သွားတယ်

Are you going there? | ho-beq thwà-mălà? | ဟိုဘက် သွားမလား။
I won't go today. | dì-né măthwà-bù | ဒီနေ့မသွားဘူး။

God	p'ăyà thăk'in	ဘုရားသခင်
good	kaùn-deh	ကောင်းတယ်
government	ăsò-yá	အစိုးရ
grandchild	myè/myì	မြေး
grandfather	ăp'ò	အဘိုး
grandmother	ăp'wà	အဘွား
greedy	làw-bá cì-deh	လောဘကြီးတယ်

grow up	cì-t'wà-deh	ကြီးထွားတယ်
guard (n)	ăsaún	အစောင့်
guard (v)	saún-deh	စောင့်တယ်
guess (v)	hmàn-s'á-deh	မှန်းဆတယ်
guest	éh-dheh	ဧည့်သည်
guide (n)	gaiq/làn-hnyun	ဂိုက်/လမ်းညွှန်
guidebook	làn-hnyun sa-ouq	လမ်းညွှန်စာအုပ်
guilty	ăpyiq shí-deh	အပြစ်ရှိတယ်
guitar	gi-ta	ဂီတာ
gun	thănaq	သေနတ်

H

hair (of body, fur)	ămwè	အမွေး
hair (of head)	zăbin	ဆံပင်
half	tăweq	တစ်ဝက်
hand	leq	လက်
handbag	leq-pwé-eiq	လက်ဆွဲအိတ်
handicrafts	leq-hmú-pyiq-sì	လက်မှုပစ္စည်း
handsome	c'àw-màw-deh	ချောမောတယ်
happy	pyaw-shwin-deh	ပျော်ရွှင်တယ်
hard (not soft)	k'ain-ma-deh	ခိုင်မာတယ်
hard (not easy)	k'eq-teh	ခက်တယ်
hat	ouq-t'ouq	ဦးထုပ်
hate (v)	moùn-fi-deh	မုန်းတီးတယ်
have	shí-deh	ရှိတယ်
I have ...	... shí-ba-deh	... ရှိပါတယ်
Have you (got) ...?	... shí-là?	... ရှိလား။
health	càn-ma-yè	ကျန်းမာရေး
hear	cà-deh	ကြားတယ်
heater	ăpu-pè-kări-ya	အပူပေးကိရိယာ
heavy	lè-deh	လေးတယ်
Hello.	min-găla-ba (lit: It's a blessing)	မင်္ဂလာပါ။

help (v)	ku-nyi-deh	ကူညီတယ်
Can I help?	ku-nyi-ba-yá-ze?	ကူညီပါရစေ။
Help!	keh-ba!	ကယ်ပါ။
here	di-hma	ဒီမှာ
heroin	bein-byu/'Number 4'	ဘိန်းဖြူ/ နံဘတ်ဖိုး
high	myín-deh	မြင့်တယ်
hill	taun-goùn	တောင်ကုန်း
hire	hngà-deh	ငှါးတယ်
I'd like to hire ...	... hngà-jin-deh	... ငှါးချင်တယ်။
history	thămàin	သမိုင်း
historical	thămàin-win-deh	သမိုင်းဝင်တယ်
hit	yaiq-teh	ရိုက်တယ်
hitchhike	kà-joun-sì-deh	ကားကြံုစီးတယ်
holiday (day off)	à-laq-yeq	အားလပ်ရက်
holy	mun-myaq-teh	မွန်မြတ်တယ်
home	ein	အိမ်
homeland/town	za-ti	ဇာတိ
homesick	ein-go lwàn-deh	အိမ်ကိုလွမ်းတယ်
homosexual (male)	mein-măsha/	မိန်းမလျာ/
	ăc'auq	အခြောက်
honest	yò-thà-deh	ရိုးသားတယ်
hope (n)	hmyaw-lín-jeq	မျှော်လင့်ချက်
hope (v)	hmyaw-lín-deh	မျှော်လင့်တယ်
horse	myìn	မြင်း
hospitality	éh-wuq	ဧည့်ဝတ်
hospital	s'è-youn	ဆေးရုံ
hot (temperature)	pu-deh	ပူတယ်
hot (spicy)	saq-teh	စပ်တယ်
hotel	ho-teh	ဟိုတယ်
hour	na-yi	နာရီ
house	ein	အိမ်
house arrest	ăceh-ăjouq	အကျယ်အချုပ်

H

D
I
C
T
I
O
N
A
R
Y

how	beh-lo	ဘယ်လို
How do I get to ...?	... go beh-lo thwà-yá-mălèh?	... ကို ဘယ်လို သွားရမလဲ။
How much is ... ?	... beh-lauq-lèh?	... ဘယ်လောက်လဲ။
How are you?	ne-kaùn-yéh-là?	နေကောင်းရဲ့လား။
How? (in what way?)	beh-lo-lèh?	ဘယ်လိုလဲ။
humanity (people)	lu-dhà	လူသား
human rights	lu-ăk'wín-ăyè	လူ့အခွင့်အရေး
hungry	baiq s'a-deh	ဗိုက်ဆာတယ်
I'm hungry.	baiq s'a-ne-deh	ဗိုက်ဆာနေတယ်။
Are you hungry?	baiq s'a-yéh-là?	ဗိုက်ဆာရဲ့လား။
hurriedly	ăyin-zălo	အလျင်စလို
hurt (pain)	na-deh	နာတယ်
husband	yauq-cà	ယောကျ်ား

I

ice	ye-gèh	ရေခဲ
identity card	hmaq-poun-tin	မှတ်ပုံတင်
if	... yin	... ရင်
ill	ne-măkaùn-bù	နေမကောင်းဘူး
illegal	ú-băde-néh mănyi-bù	ဥပဒေနဲ့မညီဘူး
imagine	seiq-kù-deh	စိတ်ကူးတယ်
imitate	ătú-k'ò-deh	အတုခိုးတယ်
immediately	c'eq-c'ìn	ချက်ချင်း
import (v)	tin-thwìn-deh	တင်သွင်းတယ်
important	ăyè-jì-deh	အရေးကြီးတယ်
impossible (no chance)	măp'yiq-nain-bù	မဖြစ်နိုင်ဘူး။
imprison	t'aun-c'á-deh	ထောင်ချတယ်
in	... hma	... မှာ
included, be	pa-deh	ပါတယ်
inconvenient	ăs'in măpye-bù	အဆင်မပြေဘူး
industry	seq-hmú-louq-ngàn	စက်မှုလုပ်ငန်း
infectious	kù-seq-taq-teh	ကူးစက်တတ်တယ်

information	dhǎdìn	သတင်း
inject (medicine)	s'è t'ò-deh	ဆေးထိုးတယ်
injury	dan-ya	ဒဏ်ရာ
insecticide	pò thaq-s'è	ပိုးသတ်ဆေး
inside	ǎtwìn	အတွင်း
insurance	a-má-k'an	အာမခံ
It's insured.	a-má-k'an shí-deh	အာမခံရှိတယ်
intelligent	nyan-t'eq-teh	ဉာဏ်ထက်တယ်
interest (money)	ǎtò	အတိုး
interested, be	seiq-win-sà-deh	စိတ်ဝင်စားတယ်
interesting	seiq-win-sà-zǎya	စိတ်ဝင်စားစရာ
	kaùn-deh	ကောင်းတယ်
international	nain-ngan-dǎga	နိုင်ငံတကာ
interpreter	zǎgǎbyan	စကားပြန်
introduce	meiq-s'eq pè-deh	မိတ်ဆက်ပေးတယ်
invite (v)	p'eiq-teh/k'aw-deh	ဖိတ်တယ်/ခေါ်တယ်
iron (metal)	than	သံ
iron (for clothes)	mì-bu	မီးပူ
iron (v)	mì-bu taiq-deh	မီးပူတိုက်တယ်
island	cùn	ကျွန်း
itchy	yà-deh	ယားတယ်

J

jail	ǎcin-daun	အကျဉ်းထောင်
jazz	jaz gi-tá	ဂျက်ဇ်ဂီတ
jeans	jìn-baùn-bi	ဂျင်းဘောင်းဘီ
jewellery	leq-wuq-leq-sà	လက်ဝတ်လက်စား
job	ǎlouq-ǎkain	အလုပ်အကိုင်
joke (n)	yi-zǎya	ရယ်စရာ
joke (v)	yi-zǎya pyàw-deh	ရယ်စရာ ပြောတယ်
jump (v)	k'oun-deh	ခုန်တယ်
just (fair)	hman-gan-deh	မှန်ကန်တယ်
justice/law	tǎyà-ú-bǎde	တရားဥပဒေ

K

keep	theìn-t'à-deh	သိမ်းထားတယ်
key	tháw	သော့
kill	thaq-teh	သတ်တယ်
kind, be	cin-na-deh	ကြင်နာတယ်
kind (type)	ămyò-ăsà	အမျိုးအစား
king	băyin/mìn	ဘုရင်/မင်း
kiss (v)	nàn-deh	နမ်းတယ်
kitchen	mì-bo-jaun	မီးဖိုချောင်
kite	le-tăgun	လေတံခွန်
knapsack	càw-pò-eiq	ကျောပိုးအိတ်
knee	dù	ဒူး
knife	dà	ဓါး
know	thí-deh	သိတယ်
I know him.	**thu-go thí-deh**	**သူ့ကို သိတယ်။**
I know that.	**èh-da thí-deh**	**အဲ့ဒါသိတယ်။**
know (how to)	... taq/daq ...	... တတ် ...
I know how to dance.	**ká-daq-teh**	**ကတတ်တယ်။**

L

lacquer (resin)	thiq-sè	သစ်စေး
lake	ain/kan/ìn	အိုင်/ကန်/အင်း
land	koùn-mye	ကုန်းမြေ
land (plane etc) (v)	s'aiq-teh	ဆိုက်တယ်
language	zăgà	စကား
last (adj)	nauq-s'oùn	နောက်ဆုံး
late	nauq-cá-deh	နောက်ကျတယ်
latest (adj)	nauq-s'oùn	နောက်ဆုံး
laugh	yi-deh	ရယ်တယ်
laundry (shop)	pìn-mìn-s'ain	ပင်မင်းဆိုင်
law	ú-băde	ဥပဒေ

L

lawyer	shé-ne	ရှေ့နေ
laxative	wùn-hnouq-s'è	ဝမ်းနှုတ်ဆေး
lazy	pyìn-deh	ပျင်းတယ်
learn	thin-deh	သင်တယ်
leather	thăye	သားရေ
leave (depart)	t'weq-teh	ထွက်တယ်
leave (behind)	can-deh	ကျန်တယ်
left (not right)	beh-beq	ဘယ်ဘက်
leg	c'e-dauq	ခြေထောက်
legal	ú-băde-néh nyi-deh	ဥပဒေနဲ့ ညီတယ်
lesbian	yauq-cà-sha	ယောက်ျားလျာ
less	po-nèh-deh	ပိုနည်းတယ်
letter	sa	စာ
letter (ABC)	eq-k'ăya	အက္ခရာ
library	sa-cí-daiq	စာကြည့်တိုက်
lie (deceive) (v)	lein-pyàw-deh	လိမ်ပြောတယ်
lice	thàn	သန်း
lid	ăp'oùn	အဖုံး
life	ătheq/băwă	အသက်/ဘဝ
lift (elevator)	daq-hle-gà	ဓာတ်လှေကား
light (weight)	páw-deh	ပေါ့တယ်
light (colour)	p'yáw-deh	ဖျော့တယ်
light switch	mì-k'ălouq	မီးခလုတ်
lightning	mò-jò	မိုးကြိုး
like (similar)	tu-deh	တူတယ်
like (v)	caiq-teh	ကြိုက်တယ်
line	myìn-jaùn	မျဉ်းကြောင်း
lip	hnouq-k'àn	နှုတ်ခမ်း
listen	nà-t'aun-deh	နားထောင်တယ်
little (adj)	ngeh-deh	ငယ်တယ်
live (v)	ne-deh	နေတယ်
lock (n)	tháw-gălauq	သော့ခလောက်
long (adj)	sheh-deh	ရှည်တယ်

D
I
C
T
I
O
N
A
R
Y

long ago (adv)	shè-doùn-gá	ရှေးတုန်က
look at (v)	cí-deh	ကြည့်တယ်
look for (v)	sha-deh	ရှာတယ်
lose (fail)	shoùn-deh	ရှုံးတယ်
It is lost.	pyauq-thwà-bi	ပျောက်သွားပြီ။
loud	ăthan ceh-deh	အသံ ကျယ်တယ်
love (v)	c'iq-teh	ချစ်တယ်
I love you.	k'ămya/	ခင်ဗျား/
	shin-go c'iq-teh (m/f)	ရှင်ကို ချစ်တယ်။
lucky	kan kaùn-deh	ကံကောင်းတယ်
lunch	né-leh-za	နေ့လယ်စာ

M

machine	seq	စက်
mad (crazy)	yù-deh	ရူးတယ်
major (army)	bo-hmù	ဗိုလ်မှူ
majority	ămyà-zú	အများစု
make	louq-teh	လုပ်တယ်
Did you make it yourself?	ko-dain louq-thălà?	ကိုယ်တိုင် လုပ်သလား။
make a bed	eiq-ya thein-deh	အိပ်ရာသိမ်းတယ်။
many	ămyà-jì	အများကြီး
map	mye-boun	မြေပုံ
marijuana	s'è-j'auq	ဆေးခြောက်
market	zè	ဈေး
marriage	ein-daun-yè	အိမ်ထောင်ရေး
marriage ceremony	mingăla-bwèh	မင်္ဂလာပွဲ
married	ein-daun shí-bi	အိမ်ထောင် ရှိပြီ
marry	leq-t'aq-teh	လက်ထပ်တယ်
massage	hneiq-teh	နှိပ်တယ်
matches	mì-jiq	မီးခြစ်
matter (issue)	keiq-sá	ကိစ္စ

It doesn't matter.	keiq-sá-mǎshí-ba-bù	ကိစ္စမရှိပါဘူး။
maybe	p'yiq-léin-meh	ဖြစ်လိမ့်မယ်
meet	twé-deh	တွေ့တယ်
I'll meet you.	k'ǎmyà/shin-néh twé-meh	ခင်ဗျား/ရှင်နဲ့ တွေ့မယ်။
mend	pyin-deh	ပြင်တယ်
message	ǎhma-zǎgà	အမှာစကား
middle, in the	ǎleh-hma	အလယ်မှာ
mind (n)	seiq	စိတ်
minister (government)	wun-jì	ဝန်ကြီး
minority	ǎnèh-zú	အနည်းစု
minute (time)	mǎniq	မိနစ်
miss (long for)	lùn-deh/lwàn-deh	လွမ်းတယ်
mistake, make a	hmà-deh	မှားတယ်
mix (v)	yàw-deh	ရောတယ်
modern	k'iq-mi-deh	ခေတ်မီတယ်
monastery	p'oùn-jì-caùn	ဘုန်းကြီး ကျောင်း
money	paiq-s'an	ပိုက်ဆံ
monkey	myauq	မျောက်
monument	ǎt'ein-ǎhmaq cauq-tain	အထိမ်းအမှတ် ကျောက်တိုင်
more (pl)	po-myà-deh	ပိုများတယ်
morning	mǎneq	မနက်
morphine	maw-p'eìn/maw-p'ì-yà	မော်ဖိန်/မော်ဖိယား
mosque	bǎli	ဗလီ
mosquito	c'in	ခြင်
mountain	taun	တောင်
mountaineering	taun teq-ta	တောင်တက်တာ
mouth	bǎzaq	ပါးစပ်
movie	youq-shin-kà	ရုပ်ရှင်ကား
mud	shún	ရွှံ့
museum	pyá-daiq	ပြတိုက်
music	thǎc'ìn	သီချင်း

N

nail (metal)	than-jaùn	သံချောင်း
name (n)	na-meh	နာမည်
name (v)	kin-bùn taq-teh	ကင်ပွန်းတပ်တယ်
narrow	cìn-deh	ကျဉ်းတယ်
national park	ămyò-dhà-ú-yin	အမျိုးသားဥယျာဉ်
nature/natural	dhăba-wá	သဘာဝ
near (adj)	nì-deh	နီးတယ်
nearby (close)	di-nà-hma	ဒီနားမှာ
necessary (adj)	măshí-măp'yiq-téh	မရှိမဖြစ်တဲ့
need (v)	lo-aq-deh	လိုအပ်တယ်
neighbour	ein-nì-jìn	အိမ်နီးချင်း
neighbourhood	yaq-kweq	ရပ်ကွက်
never (in the past)	tăk'a-hmá	တစ်ခါမှ
never (in the future)	beh-dáw-hmá	ဘယ်တော့မှ
new	ăthiq	အသစ်
news	thădìn	သတင်း
newspaper	thădìn-za	သတင်းစာ
next time	nauq-tăk'a	နောက်တစ်ခါ
nice (person)	thăbàw kaùn-deh	သဘော ကောင်းတယ်
night	nyá	ည
No.	măhouq-pa-bù	မဟုတ်ပါဘူး။
noise	ăthan	အသံ
noisy	s'u-nyan-deh	ဆူညံတယ်
none	tăk'ú-hmá	တစ်ခုမှ
normal	poun-hman p'yiq-teh	ပုံမှန် ဖြစ်တယ်
nothing	ba-hmá	ဘာမှ
not any more	măp'yiq-táw-bù	မဖြစ်တော့ဘူး။
not yet	măp'yiq-thè-bù	မဖြစ်သေးဘူး။
now	ăk'ú	အခု
nuclear energy	ănú-myu sùn-in	အဏုမြူ စွမ်းအင်
nun	thi-lá-shin	သီလရှင်
nurse (n)	thu-na-byú	သူနာပြု
nut	ăk'un-ma-dhì	အခွံမာသီး

O

obvious	t'in-shà-deh	ထင်ရှားတယ်
occasionally	tăk'a-tăk'a	တစ်ခါတစ်ခါ
occupation	ălouq-ăkain	အလုပ်အကိုင်
ocean	pin-leh	ပင်လယ်
offer (religious) (v)	hlu-deh	လှူတယ်
office	yoùn	ရုံး
officer (military)	siq-bo	စစ်ဗိုလ်
official (person)	ăya-shí	အရာရှိ
often	k'ăná-k'ăná	ခဏခဏ
oil (cooking)	s'i	ဆီ
oil (petroleum)	ye-nan	ရေနံ
oily	s'i myà-deh	ဆီများတယ်
old (of person)	ătheq-cì-deh	အသက်ကြီးတယ်
old (of thing)	haùn-deh	ဟောင်းတယ်
on	... paw-hma	... ပေါ်မှာ
once	tăk'a	တစ်ခါ
one	tiq	တစ်
open, be	pwín-deh	ပွင့်တယ်
open (something)	p'wín-deh	ဖွင့်တယ်
opinion	ăyu-ăs'á	အယူအဆ
opium	beìn	ဘိန်း
opportunity	ăk'wín	အခွင့်
opposite (adv)	myeq-hnăjìn-s'ain	မျက်နှာချင်းဆိုင်
opposition	s'án-cin-beq	ဆန့်ကျင်ဘက်
or	da-hmá măhouq-yin	ဒါမှ မဟုတ်ရင်
order (n)	ămeín	အမိန့်
order (eg, army) (v)	ămeín pè-deh	အမိန့်ပေးတယ်
order (food etc) (v)	hma-deh	မှာတယ်
ordinary	tha-man	သာမန်
organisation	ăs'ì-ăyoùn	အစည်းအရုံး
organise	si-zin-deh	စီစဉ်တယ်

original	mu-yìn	မူရင်း
orphan	mí-bá-méh kălè	မိဘမဲ့ကလေး
other	tăc'à	တခြား
outside	ăpyin-beq	အပြင်ဘက်
overnight (v)	nyá eiq-teh	ညအိပ်တယ်
overseas	nain-ngan-yaq-c'à	နိုင်ငံရပ်ခြား
owe (v)	ăcwè tin-deh	အကြွေးတင်တယ်
owner	pain-shin	ပိုင်ရှင်

P

package/packet	ăt'ouq	အထုပ်
pack of cigarettes	sì-găreq-tăt'ouq	စီးကရက်တစ်ထုပ်
paddy (rice)	zăbà	စပါး
paddy (field)	leh	လယ်
padlock	tháw-gălauq	သော့ခလောက်
page	sa-myeq-hná	စာမျက်နှာ
painful	na-jin-ze-deh	နာကျင်စေတယ်
painting	păji-kà	ပန်းချီကား
pair	tăyan/dăsoun	တစ်ရန်/တစ်စုံ
palace	nàn-daw	နန်းတော်
paper	seq-ku	စက္ကူ
parade, military	siq-yè-pyá-bwèh	စစ်ရေးပြပွဲ
parcel	pa-s'eh	ပါဆယ်
parents	mí-bá	မိဘ
park	pàn-jan	ပန်းခြံ
parliament	hluq-taw	လွှတ်တော်
parrot	ceq-tu-ywè	ကြက်တူရွေး
part (piece)	tăzeiq-/tăk'àn	တစိတ်/တခန်
participate	pa-win-deh	ပါဝင်တယ်
party (social)	pyaw-bwèh	ပျော်ပွဲ
party (political)	pa-ti	ပါတီ

party member	pa-ti ăp'wéh-win	ပါတီအဖွဲ့ဝင်
pass (mountain)	taun-jà-làn	တောင်ကြားလမ်း
pass (overtake)	caw-deh	ကျော်တယ်
passenger	k'ăyì-dheh	ခရီးသည်
passport	paq-săpó	ပတ်စပို့
path	làn	လမ်း
patriotism	myò-c'iq-seiq	မျိုးချစ်စိတ်
pay (earnings) (n)	lá-gá	လခ
pay (v)	pè-deh	ပေးတယ်
peace	nyèin-jàn-yè	ငြိမ်းချမ်းရေး
pearl	pălèh	ပုလဲ
pen	bàw-pin/kălaun	ဘောပင်/ကလောင်
people (in general)	lu-dó	လူတို့
People, The	pye-thu lu-dú	ပြည်သူလူထု
percentage	ya-g'ain-hnoùn	ရာခိုင်နှုန်း
period (time)	ka-lá	ကာလ
period, to have a	thwè-cá-deh/	သွေးကျတယ်/
	thwè-paw-deh	သွေးပေါ်တယ်
permanent	ămyèh-dàn	အမြဲတမ်း
permission	ăk'win	အခွင့်
permit (n)	pa-miq	ပါမစ်
permit (v)	k'win-pè-deh	ခွင့်ပေးတယ်
persecute	p'í-hneiq-teh	ဖိနှိပ်တယ်
person	pouq-go	ပုဂ္ဂိုလ်
personal (private)	pouq-gălí-ká	ပုဂ္ဂလိက
personality (nature)	săyaiq	စရိုက်
petrol (gasoline)	daq-s'i	ဓါတ်ဆီ
pharmacy	s'è-zain	ဆေးဆိုင်
photograph (n)	daq-poun	ဓါတ်ပုံ
photograph (v)	daq-poun yaiq-teh	ဓါတ်ပုံရိုက်တယ်
Can I take a photograph?	daq-poun yaiq-ló yá-là?	ဓါတ်ပုံရိုက်လို့ ရလား။

P

piece	ăpaìn	အပိုင်း
pilgrim	p'ăyà-p'ù	ဘုရားဖူး
pilgrimage, go on a	p'ăyà-p'ù-thwà-deh	ဘုရားဖူးသွားတယ်
pill	s'è-loùn/s'è-byà	ဆေးလုံး/ဆေးပြား
pillow	gaùn-oùn	ခေါင်းအုံး
pipe (tobacco)	s'è-dan	ဆေးတံ
place	ne-ya	နေရာ
plan (n)	ăsi-ăsin/ăcan	အစီအစဉ်/အကြံ
plane	le-yin-byan	လေယာဉ်ပျံ
plant (n)	ăpin	အပင်
plant (v)	saiq-teh	စိုက်တယ်
plate	păgan	ပန်းကန်
play (v)	găza-deh	ကစားတယ်
plug (for sink)	ăs'ó	အဆို့
plug (electric)	pălaq	ပလပ်
poem	kăbya	ကဗျာ
poetry	kăbya	ကဗျာ
point (v)	hnyun-deh	ညွှန်တယ်
poison	ăs'eiq	အဆိပ်
police	yèh	ရဲ
politics	nain-ngan-yè	နိုင်ငံရေး
pollute	nyiq-nyàn-ze-deh	ညစ်ညမ်းစေတယ်
pool (swimming)	ye-kù-gan	ရေကူးကန်
poor	s'ìn-yèh-deh	ဆင်းရဲတယ်
porter	paw-ta	ပေါ်တာ
be taken	paw-ta	ပေါ်တာ
as a porter	s'wèh-gan-yá-deh	ဆွဲခံရတယ်။
post office	sa-daiq	စာတိုက်
pot (container)	ò	အိုး
poverty	s'ìn-yèh-da	ဆင်းရဲတာ
power (influence)	àw-za	သြဇာ

D I C T I O N A R Y

practical	leq-twé-cá-deh	လက်တွေ့ကျတယ်
pray	s'ú-taùn-deh	ဆုတောင်းတယ်
prefer	po-caiq-teh	ပိုကြိုက်တယ်
pregnant	ko-wun shí-deh	ကိုယ်ဝန်ရှိတယ်
prepare	pyin-zin-deh	ပြင်ဆင်တယ်
present (time)	leq-shí	လက်ရှိ
present (gift)	leq-s'aun	လက်ဆောင်
president	thămădá	သမ္မတ
pretty	hlá-deh	လှတယ်
prevent	tà-s'í-deh	တားဆီးတယ်
price	zè-hnoùn	ဈေးနှုန်း
pride	ma-ná	မာန
prime minister	wun-jì-jouq	ဝန်ကြီးချုပ်
prison	ăcìn-daun	အကျဉ်းထောင်
prison sentence	t'aun-dan	ထောင်ဒဏ်
prisoner (m)	ăcìn-dhà	အကျဉ်းသား
prisoner (f)	ăcìn-dhu	အကျဉ်းသူ
prisoner of war	siq-thoún-bàn	စစ်သုံ့ပန်း
private (army)	siq-thà	စစ်သား
private possession	ko-bain pyiq-sì	ကိုယ်ပိုင်ပစ္စည်း
problem	pyaq-dhăna	ပြဿနာ
profit	ămyaq	အမြတ်
program	ăsi-ăsin	အစီအစဉ်
promise (n)	gădí	ကတိ
promise (v)	gădí pyú-deh	ကတိပြုတယ်
prostitute	pyé-dăza/p'a	ပြည့်တန်ဆာ/ဖာ
protect	ka-gweh-deh	ကာကွယ်တယ်
protest (demo) (n)	s'an-dá pyá-bwèh	ဆန္ဒပြပွဲ
pull	s'wèh-deh	ဆွဲတယ်
pun (v)	zăgà-p'an-t'ò-deh	စကားဖန်ထိုးတယ်
pupil (follower)	dăbyí/dăbeq	တပည့်
push	tùn-deh	တွန်းတယ်

Q

quality	ăyi-ăthwè	အရည်အသွေး
quarter (fourth)	ăseiq/lè-boún-tăboun	အစိတ်/လေ ပုံတစ်ပုံ
quarter (town)	yaq-kweq	ရပ်ကွက်
queen	băyin-má	ဘုရင်မ
question (n)	mè-gùn	မေ ခွန်
queue (v)	tàn-si-deh	တန် စီတယ်
quick	myan-deh	မြန်တယ်
quiet	è-s'è-deh	အေ ဆေ တယ်
quite, moderately	ătaw-ătan	အတော်အတန်

R

race (contest)	ăpyè-pyain-bwèh	အပြေး ပြိုင်ပွဲ
radio	re-di-yo	ရေဒီယို
railway (line)	yăt'à-làn	ရထား လမ်
rain (v)	mò	မိုး
It's raining.	mò ywa-ne-deh	မိုးရွာနေတယ်။
rape (n)	mú-dein-hmú	မုဒိမ် မှု
rape (v)	mú-dein cín-deh	မုဒိမ် ကျင့်တယ်
rare	shà-pà-deh	ရှား ပါ တယ်
rat	cweq	ကြွက်
raw	ăsein	အစိမ်
read	p'aq-teh	ဖတ်တယ်
ready	ăthín-p'yiq-teh	အသင့်ဖြစ်တယ်
reason	ăcaùn	အကြောင်
receipt	pye-za	ပြေစာ
recently	măca-gin-gá	မကြာခင်က
recommend	ăcan pè-deh	အကြံပေးတယ်
recycle	pyan-leh thoùn-deh	ပြန်လည်သုံ တယ်
referee	dain	ဒိုင်
refugee	douq-k'á-dheh	ဒုက္ခသည်

ENGLISH – BURMESE

English	Transliteration	Burmese
refund (v)	pyan-àn-deh	ပြန်အမ်းတယ်
refuse	nyìn-deh	ငြင်းတယ်
region	de-thá	ဒေသ
regulation	nì-ú-bǎde	နည်း ဥပဒေ
relatives	s'we-myò-de	ဆွေမျိုး တွေ
relax (v)	ǎnà-yu-deh	အနား ယူတယ်
religion	ba-dha-yè	ဘာသာရေး
remember (recognise)	hmaq-mí-deh	မှတ်မိတယ်
remember (think of)	dhǎdí-yá-deh	သတိရတယ်
remote	theiq-wè-deh	သိပ်ဝေးတယ်
rent (n)	hngà-gá	ငှါ ခ
rent (v)	hngà-deh	ငှါ တယ်
repeat (again)	pyan ...	ပြန် ...
Please repeat that.	pyan-pyàw-ba-oùn	ပြန်ပြောပါအုံး။
representative	ko-zǎhleh	ကိုယ်စား လှယ်
republic	thǎmǎdá nain-ngan	သမ္မတနိုင်ငံ
reserve (v)	thì-thán-t'a-deh	သီ သန့်ထား တယ်
respect (v)	lè-zà-deh	လေးစား တယ်
responsibility	ta-wun	တာဝန်
rest (v)	ǎnà-yu-deh	အနား ယူတယ်
restaurant	sa-thauq-s'ain	စား သောက်ဆိုင်
return (v)	pyan-deh	ပြန်တယ်
We'll return on ...	... pyan-la-meh	... ပြန်လာမယ်။
return ticket	ǎthwà-ǎpyan leq-hmaq	အသွား အပြန်လက်မှတ်
revolution	taw-hlan-yè	တော်လှန်ရေး
rich	c'àn-tha-deh	ချမ်း သာတယ်
rich person	thǎt'è	သူဌေး
right (not left)	nya-beq	ညာဘက်
right (correct)	hman-deh	မှန်တယ်
ripe	hméh-deh	မှည့်တယ်

risky	bè-myà-deh	ဘေးများတယ်
river	myiq	မြစ်
road	làn	လမ်း
robber ('dacoit')	dămyà	ဓါးပြ
robe (of monk)	thin-gàn	သင်္ကန်း
roof	ămò	အမိုး
room	ăk'àn	အခန်း
root	ămyiq	အမြစ်
rope	cò	ကြိုး
rotten	pouq-teh	ပုပ်တယ်
round (adj)	wàin-deh	ဝိုင်းတယ်
rubber	raw-ba	ရော်ဘာ
rubbish	ăhmaiq	အမှိုက်
rude	yàin-deh	ရိုင်းတယ်
ruins	ăpyeq-ăsì	အပျက်အစီး
rule (regulation) (n)	sì-kàn	စည်းကမ်း
rule (govern) (v)	ouq-c'ouq-teh	အုပ်ချုပ်တယ်
run	pyè-deh	ပြေးတယ်

S

sad	wùn-nèh-deh	ဝမ်းနည်းတယ်
safe (n)	mì-k'an-thiq-ta	မီးခံသေတ္တာ
safe (adj)	bè-kìn-deh	ဘေးကင်းတယ်
salary (monthly)	lá-za	လစာ
salty	s'à-ngan-deh	ဆားငန်တယ်
same	ătu-du	အတူတူ
sand	thèh	သဲ
sandbank	thaun	သောင်
sardine(tinned)	ngà-thiq-ta	ငါးသေတ္တာ
satellite	jo-dú	ဂြိုဟ်တု
say	pyàw-deh/s'o-deh	ပြောတယ်/ဆိုတယ်

| I said ... | ... ló s'o-deh | ... လို့ဆိုတယ်။ |
| Please say it again. | pyan pyàw-ba-oùn | ပြန်ပြောပါအုံး။ |

scenery	shú-hmyaw-gìn	ရှုမျှော်ခင်း
schedule	ăsi-ăsin	အစီအစဉ်
school	caùn	ကျောင်း
scissors	kaq-cì	ကတ်ကြေး
scorpion	kìn-mì-gauq	ကင်းမြီးကောက်
sea	pin-leh	ပင်လယ်
seasick (adj)	hlàin-mù-deh	လှိုင်းမူးတယ်
secret (adj)	shó-hweq-teh	လျှို့ဝှက်တယ်
see	myin-deh	မြင်တယ်

| I see (understand). | nà-leh-deh | နားလည်တယ် |
| I see (it). | ho-ha myin-deh | ဟိုဟာ မြင်တယ်။ |

selfish	kó-ăcò cí-deh	ကိုယ့်အကျိုးကြည့်တယ်
sell	yaùn-deh	ရောင်းတယ်
send	pó-deh	ပို့တယ်
sentence (words)	weq-cá	ဝါကျ
separated	k'wèh-jà-deh	ခွဲခြားတယ်
serious	lè-neq-teh	လေးနက်တယ်
sex (n)	lein	လိင်
shade (n)	ăyeiq	အရိပ်
share (n)	we-zú	ဝေစု
share (v)	k'wèh-we-deh	ခွဲဝေတယ်
shave	yeiq-teh	ရိတ်တယ်
sheet (bed)	eiq-ya-k'ìn	အိပ်ရာခင်း
shop	s'ain	ဆိုင်
shoot (gun)	pyiq-teh	ပစ်တယ်
shoot (film)	yaiq-teh	ရိုက်တယ်
short (height)	pú-deh	ပုတယ်
short (length)	to-deh	တိုတယ်
shortage	pyaq-laq-hmú	ပြတ်လပ်မှု

shout (v)	aw-deh	အော်တယ်
show (v)	pyá-deh	ပြတယ်
Show me.	cănaw/cămá-go	ကျွန်တော်/ကျွန်မကို
	pyá-ba (m/f)	ပြပါ။
shut (closed)	peiq-teh	ပိတ်တယ်
shy	sheq-teh	ရှက်တယ်
sick (unwell)	ne-măkaùn-bù	နေမကောင်းဘူ
sign (n)	ăhmaq-ăthà	အမှတ်အသာ
sign (one's name) (v)	leq-hmaq t'ò-deh	လက်မှတ်ထိုးတယ်
similar	tu-nyi-deh	တူညီတယ်
since	... gădèh-gá	... ကထည် က
sing	thăc'in-s'o-deh	သီချင်းဆိုတယ်
single (female)	ăpyo/ăpyo-jì	အပျို/အပျိုကြီး
single (male)	lu-byo/lu-byo-jì	လူပျို/လူပျိုကြီး
single (state)	ein-daun măcá-thè-bù	အိမ်ထောင်မကျသေ ဘူ ။
sink (n)	myeq-hna-thiq-kweq	မျက်နာသစ်ခွက်
sit	t'ain-deh	ထိုင်တယ်
situation	ăc'e-ăne	အခြေအနေ
size	ăyweh	အရွယ်
skin	ăye	အရေ
sky	mò-gaùn-gin	မိုးကောင်းကင်
sleep (v)	eiq-teh	အိပ်တယ်
sleepy (to be)	eiq-c'in-deh	အိပ်ချင်တယ်
slow (mentally)	hnè-deh	နေးတယ်
Please drive slowly.	p'yè-byè maùn-ba	ပြည်ပြည် မောင်းပါ။
small	ngeh-deh	ငယ်တယ်
smell (good)	hmwè-deh	မွေးတယ်
smell (bad)	nan-deh	နံတယ်
smile	pyoùn-deh	ပြုံးတယ်
snake	mwe	မြွေ

socialism	s'o-sheh-liq-săniq	ဆိုရှယ်လစ်စနစ်
soft	nú-deh	နူတယ်
soldier	siq-thà	စစ်သား
sole (of foot)	c'e-p'ăwà	ခြေဖဝါး
solid (sturdy)	k'ain-deh	ခိုင်တယ်
some	tăc'ó	တချို့
somebody	tăsoun-tăyauq	တစ်စုံတစ်ယောက်
something	tăk'ú-gú	တစ်ခုခု
sometimes	tăk'a-tăle	တစ်ခါတလေ
son	thà	သား
song	tè/thăc'in	တေး/သီချင်း
soon	măca-gin	မကြာခင်
I'm sorry.	wùn-nèh-ba-deh	ဝမ်းနည်းပါတယ်။
sound	ăthan	အသံ
souvenir	ăhmaq-tăyá	အမှတ်တရ
spa	ye-pu-sàn	ရေပူစမ်း
speak	zăgà-pyàw-deh	စကားပြောတယ်
special	ăt'ù săpeh-sheh	အထူးစပယ်ရှယ်
spider	pín-gu	ပင့်ကူ
spirit shrine	naq-kùn/naq-sin	နတ်ကွန်/နတ်စင်
spoon	zùn	ဇွန်း
sport	à-găzà	အားကစား
stairs/ladder	hle-gà	လှေခါး
stall	s'ain	ဆိုင်
stamp	tăzeiq-gaùn	တံဆိပ်ခေါင်း
standard, level	ăs'ín-ătàn	အဆင့်အတန်း
star (in sky)	kyeh	ကြယ်
state (nation)	nain-ngan	နိုင်ငံ
station	bu-da-youn	ဘူတာရုံ
stay (lodge with) (v)	tèh-deh	တည်းတယ်
stay (remain) (v)	ne-deh	နေတယ်

steal (v)	k'ò-deh	ခိုးတယ်
sting (v)	touq-teh	တုပ်တယ်
stone	cauq-toùn	ကျောက်တုံး
stop (v)	yaq-teh	ရပ်တယ်
storm	moun-dàin	မုန်တိုင်း
story (tale)	wuq-t'ú	ဝတ္ထု
straight (adv)	téh-déh	တည့်တည့်
strange	t'ù-s'àn-deh	ထူးဆန်းတယ်
stranger	lu-zèin	လူစိမ်း
street	làn	လမ်း
strike (n)	thăbeiq-hmauq-teh	သပိတ်မှောက်တယ်
string	cò	ကြိုး
strong (person)	à-shí-deh	အားရှိတယ်
study (v)	thin-deh	သင်တယ်
student (f)	caùn-dhu	ကျောင်းသူ
student (m)	caùn-dhà	ကျောင်းသား
stupid	maiq-teh	မိုက်တယ်
successful	aun-myin-deh	အောင်မြင်တယ်
suddenly	youq-tăyeq	ရုတ်တရက်
sun	ne	နေ
sunglasses	ne-ga myeq-hman	နေကာမျက်မှန်
sunrise	ne-t'weq-c'ein	နေထွက်ချိန်
sunset	ne-win-j'ein	နေဝင်ချိန်
sure	the-ja-deh	သေချာတယ်
Are you sure?	the-ja-yéh-là?	သေချာရဲ့လား။
surprised	án-àw-deh	အံ့သြတယ်
surveillance	saún-jí-da	စောင့်ကြည့်တာ
swear (curse) (v)	s'èh-deh	ဆဲတယ်
sweat (n)	c'wè	ချွေး
sweat (v)	c'wè-t'weq-teh	ချွေးထွက်တယ်
sweet (adj)	c'o-deh	ချိုတယ်
swim (v)	ye kù-deh	ရေကူးတယ်

T

table	zăbwèh	စားပွဲ
tail	mì	မြီး
tailor	aq-c'ouq-dhămà	အပ်ချုပ်သမား
take	yu-deh	ယူတယ်
I'll take one.	tăk'ú yu-meh	တစ်ခု ယူမယ်။
Can I take this?	di-tăk'ú yu-ló-yá-là?	ဒီတစ်ခု ယူလို့ရလား။
talk (v)	pyàw-deh/s'o-deh	ပြောတယ်/ဆိုတယ်
tall	ăyaq myín-deh	အရပ်မြင့်တယ်
tarmac road	kaq-tăya-làn	ကတ္တရာလမ်း
tasty	ăyá-dha shí-deh	အရသာရှိတယ်
tax	ăk'un	အခွန်
teacher	caùn-s'ăya/-má (m/f)	ကျောင်းဆရာမ
telephone (n)	(teh-li-) p'oùn	(တယ်လီ)ဖုန်း
telephone (v)	p'oùn s'eq-deh	ဖုန်းဆက်တယ်
telephone book	p'oùn làn-hnyun	ဖုန်းလမ်းညွှန်
temperature (weather)	ăpu-i'ein	အပူချိန်
temperature, have a	p'yà-deh	ဖျားတယ်
tent	mò-ga-tèh	မိုးကာတဲ
thank (v)	cè-zù tin-zăgà	ကျေးဇူး တင်စကား
	pyàw-deh	ပြောတယ်
Thanks.	cè-zù-naw/cè-zù-bèh	ကျေးဇူးနော်/ကျေးဇူးပဲ။
Thank you.	cè-zù-tin-ba-deh	ကျေးဇူးတင်ပါတယ်။
then (at that time)	ho ăc'ein-gá	ဟိုအချိန်က
then (next)	èh-di nauq	အဲဒီနောက်
there	ho-hma	ဟိုမှာ
thermos	daq-bù	ဓာတ်ဘူး
thick	t'u-deh	ထူတယ်
thief	thăk'ò	သူခိုး
thin (thing)	pà-deh	ပါးတယ်

thin (person)	pein-deh	ပိန်တယ်
thing	pyiq-sì	ပစ္စည်း
think	t'in-deh	ထင်တယ်
thirsty (to be)	ye ngaq-teh	ရေငတ်တယ်
thongs (flip-flops)	p'ănaq	ဖိနပ်
throw	pyiq-teh	ပစ်တယ်
thumb	leq-má	လက်မ
thunder (v)	mò-c'ein-deh	မိုးခြိမ်းတယ်
ticket	leq-hmaq	လက်မှတ်
tight/crowded (adj)	caq-teh	ကျပ်တယ်
time	ăc'ein	အချိန်
What time is it?	**beh ăc'ein shí-bi-lèh?**	**ဘယ်အချိန်ရှိပြီလဲ။**
timetable	ăcein-săyìn	အချိန်စာရင်း
tin can	than-bù	သံဘူး
tin can opener	p'auq-tan	ဖောက်တံ
tip (gratuity)	**dhădã-jè/bauq-s'ù**	**သဒ္ဒါကြေး/ဘောက်ဆူး**
I'm tired.	**nùn-deh/màw-deh**	**နွမ်းတယ်။/မောတယ်။**
tobacco	s'è-yweq-cì	ဆေးရွက်ကြီး
today	di-né	ဒီနေ့
together	ătu-du	အတူတူ
toilet	ein-dha	အိမ်သာ
toilet paper	ein-dha seq-ku	အိမ်သာစက္ကူ
tomorrow	măneq-p'yan	မနက်ဖြန်
tonight	di-né-nyá	ဒီနေ့ည
tongue	sha	လျှာ
too	... lèh	... လည်း
toothbrush	thăbuq-tan	သွားပွတ်တံ
toothpaste	thwà-taiq-s'è	သွားတိုက်ဆေး
toothpick	thwà-jà-t'ò-dan	သွားကြားထိုးတံ
torch (flashlight)	leq-hneiq-daq-mì	လက်နှိပ်ဓာတ်မီး
torture	hneiq-seq hnyìn-pàn-jin	နှိပ်စက်ညှင်းပန်းခြင်း

touch (contact) (v)	t'í-deh	ထိတယ်
tour (v)	k'ăyì-thwà-deh	ခရီးသွားတယ်
tourist	k'ăyì-dheh/tò-riq	ခရီးသည်/တိုးရစ်
toward	... beq-ko	... ဘက်ကို
towel	myeq-hnăthouq-păwa	မျက်နှာသုတ်ပုဝါ
town	myó	မြို့
toy	găză-zăya	ကစားစရာ
trade	koun-dhweh-yè	ကုန်သွယ်ရေး
trade union	thá-meq-gá	သမဂ္ဂ
tradition	dălé	ဓလေ့
traditional	yò-ya	ရိုးရာ
translate (spoken)	zăgà pyan-deh	စကားပြန်တယ်
translate (written)	ba-dha pyan-deh	ဘာသာပြန်တယ်
travel agency	k'ăyì-thwà-louq-ngàn	ခရီးသွားလုပ်ငန်း
tree	thiq-pin	သစ်ပင်
trek (v)	làn shauq-teh	လမ်းလျှောက်တယ်
trip	k'ăyì	ခရီး
truck (lorry)	koun-tin-kà	ကုန်တင်ကား
true	hman-deh	မှန်တယ်
trust	youn-ci-deh	ယုံကြည်တယ်
try (+ v)	... cí-deh	... ကြည့်တယ်
Try it! (food)	sà-jí-ba	စားကြည့်ပါ။
turtle	leiq	လိပ်
twice	hnăk'a/hnăs'á	နှစ်ခါ/နှစ်ဆ
typewriter	leq-hneiq-seq	လက်နှိပ်စက်

U

ugly	ăyouq s'ò-deh	အရုပ်ဆိုးတယ်
umbrella	t'ì	ထီး
uncle	ù-jì / ù-lè	ဦးကြီး/ဦးလေး
under	auq-hma	အောက်မှာ
understand	nà-leh-deh	နားလည်တယ်

I understand.	nà-leh-deh	နားလည်တယ။
I don't understand.	nà-măleh-ba-bù	နားမလည်ပါဘူး။

unemployed (adj)	ălouq-méh	အလုပ်မဲ့
United Nations	kú-lá thá-meq-gá	ကုလသမဂ္ဂ
university	teq-kătho	တက္ကသိုလ်
unsafe	măloun-joun-bù	မလုံခြုံဘူး
until	ăt'í	အထိ
up	ăt'eq-ko	အထက်ကို
upstairs	ăpaw-daq-hma	အပေါ်ထပ်မှာ
urinate	s'ì-thwà-deh	ဆီးသွားတယ်
useful	ăthoùn cá-deh	အသုံးကျတယ်

V

vaccinate	ka-gweh-s'è t'ò-deh	ကာကွယ်ဆေးထိုးတယ်
vaccine	ka-gweh-s'è	ကာကွယ်ဆေး
valium	be-li-yan	ဗေလီယံ
valley	taun-jà	တောင်ကြား
valuable	ăp'ò cì-deh	အဖိုးကြီးတယ်
value (price)	ăp'ò	အဖိုး
vegetable	hìn-dhì-hìn-yweq	ဟင်းသီးဟင်းရွက်
vegetarian (adj/n)	theq-thaq-luq	သက်သတ်လွတ်
very	theiq/ăyàn	သိပ်/အရမ်း
veteran	siq-pyan	စစ်ပြန်
view (n)	myin-gwìn	မြင်ကွင်း
village	ywa	ရွာ
visa	bi-za	ဗီဇာ
visit (v)	thwà-leh-deh	သွားလည်တယ်
vitamin	à-zè/bi-ta-min	အားဆေး/ဗိတာမင်
voice	ăthan	အသံ
volunteer	louq-à-pè-deh	လုပ်အားပေးတယ်
vomit	an-deh	အန်တယ်
vote (v)	mèh-s'an-dá pè-deh	မဲဆန္ဒပေးတယ်

ENGLISH – BURMESE

W

waist	k'à	ခါး
wait	saún-ne-deh	စောင့်နေတယ်
Wait a moment!	k'ănǎ saún-ne-ba!	ခဏစောင့်နေပါ။
waiter	zăbwèh-dò	စားပွဲထိုး
wake (someone)	hnò-deh	နှိုးတယ်
walk (v)	làn shauq-teh	လမ်းလျှောက်တယ်
wall	nan-yan	နံရံ
wallet	paiq-s'an-eiq	ပိုက်ဆံအိတ်
want (see page 29)	lo-jin-deh	လိုချင်တယ်
I want ...	cănaw/cămá ... lo-jin-deh (m/f)	ကျွန်တော်/ကျွန်မ ... လိုချင်တယ်။
Do you want ...?	... lo-jin-dhălà?	... လိုချင်သလား။
war	siq	စစ်
warm (clothes)	nwè-deh	နွေးတယ်
wash (oneself)	ye-c'ò-deh	ရေချိုးတယ်
I want to bathe.	ye-c'ò-jin-ba-deh	ရေချိုးချင်ပါတယ်။
wash (clothes, hair)	shaw-deh	လျှော်တယ်
My clothes need to be washed.	ăwuq shaw-yá-meh	အဝတ်လျှော်ရမယ်။
watch (v)	cí-deh	ကြည့်တယ်
watch (timepiece)	leq-paq-na-yi	လက်ပတ်နာရီ
water	ye	ရေ
waterfall	ye-dăgun	ရေတံခွန်
wax	p'ăyaùn	ဖယောင်း
way (manner) (n)	nì	နည်း
weak	in-à măshí-bù	အင်အားမရှိဘူး
wear	wuq-teh	ဝတ်တယ်
weather	mò-le-wáthá	မိုးလေဝသ
weave	yeq-teh	ရက်တယ်
week	tăpaq	တစ်ပတ်
weight	ălè-j'ein	အလေးချိန်

201

DICTIONARY

well (n)	ye-dwìn	ရေတွင်း
wet	so-deh	စိုတယ်
what	ba	ဘာ
What time is it?	beh ǎc'ein-shí-bi-lèh?	ဘယ်အချိန်ရှိပြီလဲ။
What did you say?	ba pyàw-dhǎlèh?	ဘာပြောသလဲ။
wheel	bein	ဘီး
when (in past)	beh-doùn-gá	ဘယ်တုန်းက
When did you arrive in Myanmar?	Myǎma-pye beh-doùn-gá yauq-thǎlèh?	မြန်မာပြည် ဘယ်တုန်းက ရောက်သလဲ။
when (in future)	beh-dáw	ဘယ်တော့
When is the next boat?	nauq-thìn-bàw beh-dàw-lèh?	နောက်သင်္ဘော ဘယ်တော့လဲ။
where	beh-hma	ဘယ်မှာ
Where is ... ?	... beh-hma-lèh?	... ဘယ်မှာလဲ။
who	bǎdhu	ဘယ်သူ
Who do I ask?	bǎdhú-go mè-yá-dhǎlèh?	ဘယ်သူ့ကို မေးရသလဲ။
wide	ceh-deh	ကျယ်တယ်
widow	mouq-s'ò-má	မုဆိုးမ
widower	mouq-s'ò-bo	မုဆိုးဖို
wife	zǎnì/mǎyà	ဇနီး/မယား
win	nain-deh	နိုင်တယ်
window	bǎdìn-bauq	ပြတင်းပေါက်
wing	taun-ban	တောင်ပံ
wise	pyin-nya shí-deh	ပညာ ရှိတယ်
wish (n)	s'ú	ဆု
wish (v)	s'ú taùn-deh	ဆုတောင်းတယ်
with	... néh	... နဲ့
within	ǎt'èh-hma	အထဲမှာ
wood	thiq-thà	သစ်သား

wool	thò-mwè	သိုးမွှေး
work (n)	ălouq	အလုပ်
work (v)	ălouq-louq-teh	အလုပ်လုပ်တယ်
world	găba	ကမ္ဘာ
worse	po-s'ò-deh	ပိုဆိုးတယ်
write	yè-deh	ရေးတယ်
wrong	hmà-deh	မှားတယ်

Y

yawn (v)	thàn-deh	သမ်းတယ်
year	hniq	နှစ်
Yes.	houq-kéh	ဟုတ်ကဲ့။
yesterday	măné-gá	မနေ့က
young	ngeh-deh	ငယ်တယ်

Z

zero	thoun-nyá	သုည
zone	ăpàin	အပိုင်း
zoo	tăreiq-s'an-youn	တိရစ္ဆာန်ရုံ

INDEX

SHOULD YOU VISIT MYANMAR?

The arguments for and against travel to Myanmar are often emotional, but the choices are not black and white. The question of whether informed tourism helps or hinders the restoration of democracy and human rights in Myanmar is the subject of ongoing debate both in and out of the country.

Myanmar remains under the tight military rule of the State Peace & Development Council (SPDC), formerly known as the State Law & Order Restoration Council (SLORC), the abominable military junta that has run Myanmar since 1962. (Upon the advice of a Washington PR firm, it recently changed its name to the less catchy SPDC.) Dissent of any sort is suppressed, and political prisoners are jailed for expressing their opinions publicly. Crimes have ranged from telling jokes to owning unregistered fax machines. Several people have died in custody. Forced labour is still practised in Myanmar. It is disturbingly common in small towns and on isolated roads to see gangs of teenage girls and boys doing road work in 10-hour shifts for nothing more than meal money. There are also many reliable reports of villagers being forced to be porters for the army in warring border areas. The Burmese government has an appalling human-rights record.

Nobel Peace Prize Laureate and National League for Democracy (NLD) leader Aung San Suu Kyi advocates boycotting all forms of travel to the country, as do several activist groups outside Myanmar, as a means of isolating the government and forcing reform. Inside Myanmar, there are a number of people who support her stance on this. (It should be noted that Aung San Suu Kyi herself has been in negotiations with the junta since late 2000.) This pro-boycott group argues that much of the money from tourism goes directly into the pockets of the very generals who continue to deny Burmese citizens the most basic civil rights. Every tourist that enters Myanmar has to change a set sum of overseas funds (currently US$200) into Foreign Exchange Certificates (FECs), from which the military earns a small commission. This is one way the junta have of directly obtaining hard currency.

However, others involved with Burmese politics, including many current or former members of the NLD, feel that a travel boycott of Myanmar is counterproductive, arguing that socially responsible travel in Myanmar can be of benefit to the Burmese. The pro-travel group points out that since socialist policies were abandoned in 1989, the lot of the average Burmese has improved. They note that economic survival was the main issue of the 1988 riots that resulted in over 3000 deaths. Since the package tour requirement was waived in 1993, the potential for ordinary people to benefit from tourism has increased.

During the government's feeble 1997 Visit Myanmar campaign, the National Coalition Government of the Union of Burma (NCGUB), formed by refugee MPs who were elected in 1990 but prevented from taking office, gave this advice: 'Tourists should not engage in activities that will only benefit SLORC's coffers and not the people of Burma. However, responsible individuals and organisations who wish to verify the facts and to publicise the plight of the Burmese people are encouraged to utilise SLORC's more relaxed tourist policies'. In 2000, however, the NCGUB adopted a pro-boycott stance.

Other long-time observers in Myanmar maintain tourism is not only economically helpful but vital to the pro-democracy movement for the two-way flow of information it provides. Aung San Suu Kyi, on the other hand, regards tourism for the purpose of exchanging views on democracy as virtually useless. She has dismissed as 'patronising' the argument that tourists can teach something to the Burmese about their own plight. However, until the country began opening up to international investment and tourism in 1989, almost no one in the international community seemed to care about what had been going on inside Myanmar for the last 35 years. Myanmar's admission to the Association of Southeast Asian Nations (ASEAN) in 1997 has continued to focus regional and world attention on its investment and trade policies.

Some pro-travel observers say that international isolation has only made Myanmar's government more reliant on China (for arms and trade) and Golden Triangle drug traffickers (for the money to pay for armaments). The NCGUB's historical account states: 'The military in Burma first seized power in 1962. It expropriated all private businesses, drove out all foreigners and isolated the country from the outside world. In three decades, the military transformed a prosperous and peaceful country into a strife-torn Least Developed Country'. Further isolation may not be effective against such a government.

In fact, keeping the Burmese isolated from international witnesses to internal oppression may only cement the government's ability to rule. Forced labour was used during the restoration of the Mandalay Palace before its completion in 1997, but discontinued shortly after foreign visitors began reporting the practice to the outside world.

Anyone contemplating a visit to Myanmar should realise there are no clear-cut answers. Nevertheless, tourism remains one of the few industries to which ordinary people have access. Any reduction in tourism automatically means a reduction in local income-earning opportunities. Many Burmese citizens eke out a living from tourism, however small.

If people decide to visit Myanmar, they should support non-government tourism, and they should go with as much advance information as possible, travelling with their eyes and ears open. After decades of nothing but government propaganda, the Burmese people are insatiably curious about the rest of the world. Lonely Planet is committed to providing an independent source of information about the country which can potentially help Burmese businesses and Burmese people in general.

Every traveller must make his or her own decision. If you like the country and want to help its people, contact the organisations listed below, whether you go or not.

If you do go and would like to maximise the positive effects of a visit among the general populace, while minimising support of the government, follow these simple tactics:

- Stay at private, locally owned hotels and guesthouses, rather than in government-owned hotels. (Many new business enterprises are 'joint ventures' between the Burmese government and private firms.)
- Avoid package tours connected with Myanmar Travel & Tours (MTT; the state tourist agency). Many independent tour agencies are available in Yangon.
- Avoid MTT-sponsored modes of transport, such as the Yangon-Mandalay Express trains, the MTT ferry between Mandalay and Bagan, and Myanma Airways (MA) flights.
- Use ordinary public transport (including some private trains and many flights).

- Buy handicrafts directly from the artisans, rather than from government shops.
- Avoid patronising companies involved with military-owned Myanmar Economic Holdings. Companies with solid links to the Tatmadaw (armed forces) are often called Myawadi or Myawaddy.
- Bring a few popular (but not politically sensitive) paperback books or recent magazines to give to Burmese people. Books and magazines are often expensive or hard to find in cash-poor Myanmar, and this simple act will be much appreciated.
- Write to the Myanmar government and to the Myanmar embassy in your country expressing your views about the human-rights situation there.

Useful addresses and Web sites (many of these Web sites also contain useful links offering more information about Myanmar):

Amnesty International 1 Easton St, London WC1X 0DW; email amnestyis@amnesty.org; Web site www.amnesty.org

Bangkok Post Web site www.bangkokpost.co.th

Burma Action Group 3rd floor, Bickerton House, 25-27 Bickerton Rd, London N19 5JT; Web site www.burmacampaign.org.uk

Democratic Voice of Burma (radio) Web site www.communique.no/dvb

Free Burma Coalition Web site www.freeburmacoalition.org

Human Rights Watch Web site www.hrw.or

Karen Human Rights Group (KHRG) Web site www.khrg.org

Open Society Institute Burma Project Web site www.soros.org/burma

Partners Web site www.partnersworld.org. Charity highlighting and aiding the plight of Burmese refugees.

NOTES

Phrasebooks

L onely Planet phrasebooks are packed with essential words and phrases to help travellers communicate with the locals. With colour tabs for quick reference, an extensive vocabulary and use of script, these handy pocket-sized language guides cover day-to-day travel situations.

- handy pocket-sized books
- easy to understand Pronunciation chapter
- clear & comprehensive Grammar chapter
- romanisation alongside script to allow ease of pronunciation
- script throughout so users can point to phrases for every situation
- full of cultural information and tips for the traveller

'...vital for a real DIY spirit and attitude in language learning'
– *Backpacker*

'the phrasebooks have good cultural backgrounders and offer solid advice for challenging situations in remote locations'
– *San Francisco Examiner*

Arabic (Egyptian) • Arabic (Moroccan) • Australian *(Australian English, Aboriginal and Torres Strait languages)* • Baltic States *(Estonian, Latvian, Lithuanian)* • Bengali • Brazilian • Burmese • British *(English, dialects, Scottish Gaelic, Welsh)* • Cantonese • Central Asia *(Kazakh, Kyrgyz, Pashto, Tajik, Tashkorghani, Turkmen, Uyghur, Uzbek & others)* • Central Europe *(Czech, German, Hungarian, Polish, Slovak, Slovene)* • Costa Rica Spanish • Eastern Europe *(Albanian, Bulgarian, Croatian, Czech, Hungarian, Macedonian, Polish, Romanian, Serbian, Slovak, Slovene)* • East Timor *(Tetun, Portuguese)* • Egyptian Arabic • Ethiopian *(Amharic)* • Europe *(Basque, Catalan, Dutch, French, German, Greek, Irish, Italian, Maltese, Portuguese, Scottish Gaelic, Spanish, Turkish, Welsh)* • Farsi *(Persian)* • Fijian • French • German • Greek • Hebrew • Hill Tribes *(Lahu, Akha, Lisu, Mong, Mien & others)* • Hindi/Urdu • Indonesian • Italian • Japanese • Korean • Lao • Latin American Spanish • Malay • Mandarin • Mongolian • Moroccan Arabic • Nepali • Papua New Guinea • Pidgin • Pilipino (Tagalog) • Polish • Portuguese • Quechua • Russian • Scandinavian *(Danish, Faroese, Finnish, Icelandic, Norwegian, Swedish)* • South-East Asia *(Burmese, Indonesian, Khmer, Lao, Malay, Tagalog Pilipino, Thai, Vietnamese)* • South Pacific *(Fijian, Hawaiian, Kanak languages, Maori, Niuean, Rapanui, Rarotongan Maori, Samoan, Tahitian, Tongan & others)* • Spanish *(Castilian, also includes Catalan, Galician & Basque)* • Sri Lanka • Swahili • Thai • Tibetan • Turkish • Ukrainian • USA *(US English, vernacular, Native American, Hawaiian)* • Vietnamese

COMPLETE LIST OF LONELY PLANET BOOKS

INDIAN SUBCONTINENT Bangladesh • Bhutan • Delhi • Goa • Healthy Travel Asia & India • India • Indian Himalaya • Karakoram Highway • Kerala • Mumbai (Bombay) • Nepal • Pakistan • Rajasthan • Read This First: Asia & India • South India • Sri Lanka • Tibet • Trekking in the Indian Himalaya • Trekking in the Karakoram & Hindukush • Trekking in the Nepal Himalaya

ISLANDS OF THE INDIAN OCEAN Madagascar &Comoros • Maldives • Mauritius, Réunion & Seychelles

MIDDLE EAST & CENTRAL ASIA Bahrain, Kuwait & Qatar • Central Asia • Dubai • Iran • Israel & the Palestinian Territories • Istanbul • Istanbul to Cairo on a Shoestring • Istanbul to Kathmandu • Jerusalem • Jordan • Lebanon • Middle East • Oman & the United Arab Emirates • Syria • Turkey • World Food Turkey • Yemen

NORTH AMERICA Alaska • Boston • Boston Condensed • British Colombia • California & Nevada • California Condensed • Canada • Chicago • Deep South • Florida • Great Lakes • Hawaii • Hiking in Alaska • Hiking in the USA • Honolulu • Las Vegas • Los Angeles • Louisiana & The Deep South • Miami • Montreal • New England • New Orleans • New York City • New York City Condensed • New York, New Jersey & Pennsylvania • Oahu • Out to Eat – San Francisco • Pacific Northwest • Puerto Rico • Rocky Mountains • San Francisco • San Francisco Map • Seattle • Southwest • Texas • Toronto • USA • Vancouver • Virginia & the Capital Region • Washington DC • World Food Deep South, USA • World Food New Orleans

NORTH-EAST ASIA Beijing • China • Hiking in Japan • Hong Kong • Hong Kong Condensed • Hong Kong, Macau & Guangzhou • Japan • Korea • Kyoto • Mongolia • Seoul • Shanghai • South-West China • Taiwan • Tokyo • World Food – Hong Kong

SOUTH AMERICA Argentina, Uruguay & Paraguay • Bolivia • Brazil • Buenos Aires • Chile & Easter Island • Colombia • Ecuador & the Galapagos Islands • Healthy Travel Central & South America • Peru • Read This First: Central & South America • Rio de Janeiro • Santiago • South America on a shoestring • Santiago • Trekking in the Patagonian Andes • Venezuela

SOUTH-EAST ASIA Bali & Lombok • Bangkok • Cambodia • Hanoi • Healthy Travel Asia & India • Ho Chi Minh City • Indonesia • Indonesia's Eastern Islands • Jakarta • Java • Laos • Malaysia, Singapore & Brunei • Myanmar (Burma) • Philippines • Read This First: Asia & India • Singapore • South-East Asia on a shoestring • Thailand • Thailand's Islands & Beaches • Thailand, Vietnam, Laos & Cambodia Road Atlas • Vietnam • World Food Thailand • World Food Vietnam

Also available; Journeys travel literature, illustrated pictorials, calendars, diaries, Lonely Planet maps and videos. For more information on these series and for the complete range of Lonely Planet products and services, visit our website at **www.lonelyplanet.com**.

LONELY PLANET

Series Description

travel guidebooks	in depth coverage with backgournd and recommendations
	download selected guidebook Upgrades at www.lonelyplanet.com
shoestring guides	for travellers with more time than money
condensed guides	highlights the best a destination has to offer
citySync	digital city guides for Palm TM OS
outdoor guides	walking, cycling, diving and watching wildlife
phrasebooks	don't just stand there, say something!
city maps and road atlases	essential navigation tools
world food	for people who live to eat, drink and travel
out to eat	a city's best places to eat and drink
read this first	invaluable pre-departure guides
healthy travel	practical advice for staying well on the road
journeys	travel stories for armchair explorers
pictorials	lavishly illustrated pictorial books
eKno	low cost international phonecard with e-services
TV series and videos	on the road docos
web site	for chat, Upgrades and destination facts
lonely planet images	on line photo library

LONELY PLANET OFFICES

Australia
Locked Bag 1, Footscray,
Victoria 3011
☎ 03 8379 8000
fax 03 8379 8111
email: talk2us@lonelyplanet.com.au

UK
10a Spring Place,
London NW5 3BH
☎ 020 7428 4800
fax 020 7428 4828
email: go@lonelyplanet.co.uk

USA
150 Linden St, Oakland,
CA 94607
☎ 510 893 8555
TOLL FREE: 800 275 8555
fax 510 893 8572
email: info@lonelyplanet.com

France
1 rue du Dahomey,
75011 Paris
☎ 01 55 25 33 00
fax 01 55 25 33 01
email: bip@lonelyplanet.fr
website: www.lonelyplanet.fr

**World Wide Web: www.lonelyplanet.com or AOL keyword: lp
Lonely Planet Images: lpi@lonelyplanet.com.au**